PROFESSIONAL AWARENESS IN
SOFTWARE ENGINEERING

PROFESSIONAL AWARENESS IN SOFTWARE ENGINEERING
Or should a software engineer wear a suit?

Edited by
Colin Myers

McGRAW-HILL BOOK COMPANY

London · New York · St Louis · San Francisco · Auckland
Bogotá · Caracas · Lisbon · Madrid · Mexico
Milan · Montreal · New Delhi · Panama · Paris · San Juan
São Paulo · Singapore · Sydney · Tokyo · Toronto

Published by
McGRAW-HILL Book Company Europe
Shoppenhangers Road, Maidenhead, Berkshire, SL6 2QL, England
Telephone 01628 23432
Fax 01628 770224

British Library Cataloguing in Publication Data
Professional Awareness in Software Engineering:
   Or should a software engineer wear a suit?
I. Myers, Colin
005.1023

ISBN 0-07-707837-3

Library of Congress Cataloging-in-Publication Data
Professional Awareness in Software Engineering:
   Or should a software engineer wear a suit?
[edited by] Colin Myers.
   p.   cm.
ISBN 0-07-707837-3
1. Software Engineering.   I. Myers, Colin.
QA76.758.P759   1995
005.1'023- -dc20   94-45888
                                                        CIP

Cover design by Colin Myers, based on a drawing by Franciszka Themerson
for Bertrand Russell's *The Good Citizen's Alphabet* (1953), © Themerson
Archive, 12 Belsize Park Gardens, London, NW3 4LD.

2345 BL 9876

Typeset by Colin Myers
and printed and bound in Great Britain by Biddles Ltd., Guildford, Surrey.

Printed on permanent paper in compliance with ISO Standard 9706.

PROFESSIONAL AWARENESS IN SOFTWARE ENGINEERING

CONTENTS

PREFACE

There is an increasing concern by professional bodies and the computing industry that software engineers should be *aware* of their professional environment. This includes a need for software engineers to design their programs with both other professionals and end-users in mind, to conduct themselves in a professional manner, and also to be more aware of the legal and social implications of their product. Unfortunately, many software engineers have difficulty in appreciating the importance of these issues and most academic and training courses concentrate on technical detail. To a limited extent, general purpose management and communication courses help correct this imbalance but do not focus on the specific impact of computing and the particular problems of software engineers.

This book comprises a collection of essays which attempt to fill gaps between the technical requirements of the software engineer and the broader principles of professionalism in industry. As such, it is intended to highlight the role of the software engineer in the following areas:

◇ Software engineers and the law
◇ Software engineers and people
◇ Software engineers and software engineering

The authors come from a diverse background in software engineering practice and education; they do not necessarily agree with each other nor with the editor. The editor thinks this diversity is an advantage.

Acknowledgments

This book evolved from a series of workshops, guest lectures, seminars and student presentations on the MSc in Software Engineering at the University of Westminster. I would like to thank all those concerned, and in particular John Madsen, Dave Pitt and Wendy Stokes. Also many thanks to Eddie Kon and McGraw-Hill's Rupert Knight and Ros Comer for their patience and assistance.

Finally, this book is dedicated to the memory of my colleague and friend, Will Richardson. Will was always willing to give (sound) advice and assistance, except once when I asked to borrow his briefcase. He assured me there were two things in this world that he had never possessed: one was a briefcase; the other I shall now never know.

CHAPTER ONE

A SUITABLE PROFESSION
BY COLIN MYERS

1.1 Introduction

This chapter outlines the diverse reactions of people towards the computing industry. First, it looks at the polarization of attitudes of people who are not computer literate, and how they view software engineers. It then looks at the attitudes of software engineers and asks the question whether software engineering can or should be considered a profession. As such this chapter serves as a general introduction to the rest of the book.

1.2 Attitudes towards computers

Perhaps the most important aspect of "professional awareness" is for the "professional" to be aware that the rest of the world is not part of their profession. This is especially significant for software engineers in that they belong to a new profession and that there is still substantial mistrust and ignorance of information technology amongst the general public. Perhaps the range of attitudes towards computer technology can best be polarized by two examples taken from the realm of science fiction:

◇ The computer as an omnipotent threat
◇ The computer as friend and ally

1.2.1 The computer as an omnipotent threat

In 1954, Frederic Brown wrote a one page short story called *Answer*. It begins with the integration of all the "computing machines" of all the universe's ninety-six billion planets into one combined "cybernetics machine". The protagonist, Dwar Ev, turns the machine on and is entitled to ask the first question: "Is there a God?". The machine answers without hesitation: "Yes, *now* there is a God." Dwar Ev panics, but before he can turn the machine off: "A bolt of lightning from the cloudless sky struck him down and fused the switch shut."

This literary technophobia is echoed in reality by the Members of the Exclusive Brethren (an austere Christian sect) who apparently demand that their children be exempt from compulsory teaching about computers in schools, because they believe that they are *the work of the Devil*.

Whilst not so extreme, there are considerable legitimate fears about the social and economic impact of computers [Carlsson with Leger, 1990]. For example, computers creating unemployment, de-skilling individuals, acting as Big Brother, being a source of untraceable pornography, creating illiteracy and addiction to electronic games, generating unrealistic bills and tax demands, and giving rise to uncontrollable disasters (such as the Three Mile Island nuclear-plant crisis).

1.2.2 The computer as friend and ally

By contrast, Richard Brautigan's whimsical poem *All Watched Over by Machines of Loving Grace* [Brautigan, 1968] begins:

> I like to think (and
> the sooner the better!)
> of a cybernetic meadow
> where mammals and computers
> live together in mutually
> programming harmony
> like pure water
> touching clear sky.

Here, the view is that computers are or will very soon be our allies, they will or do remove the drudgery from human existence, improve the quality of life and open up new creative opportunities.

Inevitably, many software engineers take the Brautigan stance. This is necessary for their own self-respect: it would be very hard for them to believe that they are not doing worthwhile jobs. Unfortunately, this can often have a blinkering effect: software engineers know that computers are a good thing — therefore everybody knows!

Given that the general public does not necessarily *know* that computers and computer people are desirable, it is even more important that individual software engineers are aware of their actions, and take responsibility as potential representatives of all software engineers. Of course, this is easier said than done, the technology is new and rapidly changing and is only part of a wider environment, which has its problems and hidden agendas.

1.3 How others see us

In Chapter 5 of this book, Hilary Husband in *Pity the Poor User* looks at the reactions of users to a new computer system and the potential hostility that such a system can create. This hostility is generally directed towards the computer: curiously, public attitudes towards the software engineer are not normally so hostile. Often, there exists an unrealistic reverence. This is illuminated in the sort of interaction experienced by computing professionals at a party.

Generally, I don't tell people that I work with computers for one of three reasons:

1. The Mr Spock syndrome
2. The Helpdesk syndrome
3. The Anorak syndrome

1.3.1 The Mr Spock syndrome

People who know little about how software is developed often have the belief that you must be incredibly intelligent to have anything to do with computers. This means that you are too intelligent to talk to them or to understand the idea of having a good time. You must be a boring mathematical genius.

1.3.2 The Helpdesk syndrome

On being told that you have something to do with computers, you are immediately pounced upon as the ideal person to advise on some hardware purchase, fix the malfunctioning printer driver or give advice on some arcane piece of software. The false assumption is that if you know something about computers you must know everything. When computer-innocents are informed that there are lacunae in your knowledge they believe either that you are deliberately not telling them the truth or that you are somehow unworthy. This is a general problem for any professional; solicitors are expected to know about every law, doctors about every illness. Ignorance of one aspect is unfairly extrapolated to ignorance about every aspect.

1.3.3 The Anorak syndrome

This syndrome appears in two forms. Its mildest form is that of the amateur cornering you and trying to interest you in their computer-related obsession; for example, an adventure game, theories about virtual reality or ways of dealing with computer viruses. On the whole, this is really boring. It is also symptomatic of the day-to-day problems of dealing with clients, who have enough knowledge to interfere. The danger is to make the arrogant assumption that the user can make no sensible observations.

The more severe form of the syndrome is encountered when two or more dedicated software engineers collide. A quote from Tracy Kidder's *The Soul of a New Machine* [Kidder, 1983] summarizes this problem:

> When he went to some of the parties that members of the Eclipse Group threw, he found himself and most everyone around him talking about computers. That was nothing new, but now he also found himself thinking: "This is a party. We're not supposed to be talking about work."

It is too easy to become too narrow in focus. Given that most software engineers are involved with end-user applications, they *need* a broader perspective; to some extent they should be able to place themselves in the position of their victims.

1.3.4 Surely, you don't work with computers?

Ridiculous, though it may be, I am relatively privileged (and sometimes flattered) to be treated with awe as someone who works with computers. For example, I have one client who behaves as if my very presence will cure program bugs! Other people encounter quite different reactions. In particular, a former student of mine, who is an Asian woman, has met with disbelief and hostility. Disbelief that an Asian woman could actually do something "so hard". Hostility, as a consequence of shattered preconceptions. Unfortunately, many people in our society perceive the computing profession to be a nicely white, male and middle-class profession. This misconception is explored further in Gillian Lovegrove's contribution in relation to women (Chapter 8). Much of what she has to say is also relevant to ethnic groups and to the physically disadvantaged. Sadly, the spirit of equal opportunities is not yet prevalent within the software engineering profession.

1.4 How we see ourselves

As members of a new discipline, software engineers share the arrogance of new disciples. This attitude is a necessity — without the self-belief that the untried can be tried, little progress will be made. However, this arrogance is dangerous when software engineers assume that they are always right, that they know all the answers, and that they can discard an old solution in the light of the latest innovation. They ignore the collective wisdom and experience of the outside world; in consequence, they and the outside world suffer accordingly. Regrettably, this has been demonstrated too frequently with avoidable software disasters such as the London Stock Exchange Taurus project (with a spectacular failure to anticipate loading) and the London Ambulance system (with a sad failure to run the old and new systems in tandem for a transition period). Yet, however dramatic and tragic these disasters may be, it is the quotidian attitude of the computing industry that causes more concern. The industry has a poor track record both in providing products that are fit for purpose and also in meeting deadlines. This is compounded by a lack of awareness of what can be expected from its practitioners.

1.4.1 Let's walk down Quality Street

Harold Thimbleby, in his excellent article *You're right about the cure: don't do that* [Thimbleby, 1990], is concerned about the frequent complacency of the computing industry towards software flaws or bugs. He muses:

> ... manuals warn the user not to do one thing, and then suggest remedies. I am often left wondering why the computer cannot fix a problem for the user if the manual writers knew how to do it! The complete denial of responsibility in most software warranties also speaks for the low quality standards that are widely accepted.
>
> ... If you are a user and you experience a bug, you are told the cure is simply not do it again.

Too often, the computing industry is willing to hide behind the complexity of the programming task, and allow itself to sell an inferior product with appalling documentation. A comparison can be made with the chocolate manufacturing industry. If I were to buy a box of chocolates which contained two rotten chocolates, I would return it and expect a complete refund or another box of edible chocolates. Indeed, I would have this right in law. More often than not, I would also receive a sincere apology (poor consumer relationships = poor sales) and perhaps an extra box as compensation. By contrast, if I buy a software package and detect a fault, I will be told that the manufacturers know about this and that it will probably be fixed in the next release. As a special privilege, because I have already purchased one version, I will be entitled to purchase the next upgrade at a modest reduction. With increasing product maturity and choice, I believe that this arrogance cannot continue. Nonetheless, there is still considerable resistance to providing a better product as discussed in Tracy Hall's contribution *Confessions of a Software Quality Addict* (Chapter 9).

1.4.2 The Tower of Babel project revisited

In Frederic Brooks' classic *The Mythical Man Month* [Brooks, 1975] we are given the following management audit of the *Tower of Babel* project:

> According to the Genesis account, the tower of Babel was man's second major engineering undertaking, after Noah's ark. Babel was the first engineering fiasco.
>
> The story is deep and instructive on several levels. Let us, however, examine it purely as an engineering project, and see what management lessons can be learned. How well was their project equipped with the prerequisites for success? Did they have:
>
> 1. A *clear mission?* Yes, although naively impossible. The project failed long before it ran into this fundamental limitation.
> 2. *Manpower?* Plenty of it.
> 3. *Materials?* Clay and asphalt are abundant in Mesopotamia.
> 4. Enough *time?* Yes, there is no hint of any time constraint.
> 5. Adequate *technology?* Yes, the pyramidal or conical structure is inherently stable and spreads the compressive load well. Clearly masonry was well understood. The project failed before it hit technological limitations.
>
> Well, if they had all of these things, why did the project fail?

I presented a final year undergraduate class with this situation and question, expecting the normal blank reaction but received the following answer:

Lack of planning permission!

Brooks' answer was a more prosaic *lack of communication* and consequent *lack of organization*. With regards to self-awareness, both Brooks' answer and my student's answer show that software engineers can learn from other professions. Brooks makes the vital point that when software engineering is a team task it needs to be managed as such. My student emphasized the need to explore the broader context.

This latter point is part of the approach taken by practitioners of Checkland's Soft Systems Methodology [Checkland, 1981; Checkland and Scholes, 1990]. In Checkland's *Weltanschauung* there is a need to be aware not only of the participants within the proposed system (in terms of its actors, clients and owners) but also of the external environment within which the system lies. Checkland quite rightly also points out that any would-be "problem-solver" must also take into consideration the non-technical context; that is, the impact of the analysts' intervention, local politics and social interactions within the company.

1.4.3 The market place

Of course, software engineering is not a homogenous profession. There are many different tasks and they can appear, disappear and reappear with disconcerting frequency. Often, it is not easy to evaluate what is the appropriate payment for a job nor what skills are required. This book looks at these problems in the chapters by Mark Priestley, Wendy Stokes and Terry Twomey (Chapters 11, 6 and 10). However, it is worth noting that the industry often has curious expectations and fluctuating skill requirements.

One small but significant example of the immaturity of the profession is demonstrated by the fact that it is not uncommon to see the most optimistic of adverts for software engineers. For example, a recent job advertised in conjunction with the University of Westminster sought the following skills: UNIX, SQL, SSADM, C++, Windows, Networking, and Project management. It was expected to attract a recent graduate and offered a salary of around £15 000. Whilst this was a good graduate starting salary, the diverse collection of skills is an unrealistic wish-list. A more mature profession would have been able to offer a more mature job description.

To determine what skills are actually required is even more of a problem in a profession with rapidly changing technologies. One whimsical but frequently asked question is:

What will happen when all the old Assembler programmers die?

There are two tempting answers:

1. Assembler programming will become a very desirable skill — a situation that is contrary to the expectations of the current trend in academic curricula.
2. All the old Assembler programs die. In this case, the infant art of reverse engineering will have become a science.

In either case, it can be seen that it is a non-trivial matter to anticipate skills requirements. However, the shift in the employment market makes guessing right that much more important. Over the years, larger companies have taken to employing smaller software engineering workforces. They will hire expensive specialists on a needs-must basis, for example to install a new computer network or do the top-level analysis and design of a new system. Similarly, they will hire people with relatively low-level common skills (for example, SQL or C programmers) to work as drones on a particular project and to be discarded when no longer needed rather than kept on the payroll. Of course, some people must be retained for continuity's sake — these are the network managers, the database administrators etc. The others must take responsibility for their own training and worth.

1.5 Should a software engineer wear a suit?

The working title of this book has been the above subtitle. In a way, this highlights the question of whether software engineering is a profession or an applied technology, and what attitudes are required for a software engineer to succeed as a professional.

For example, when this book was first suggested, a sceptical reviewer was worried that the subtitle implied that only men could be software engineers. I suggest that this was a rather out-dated view of suits: I know of one female software engineer who has enviable green padded shoulders on her suits. Perhaps more seriously, the sceptic believed that the issues addressed were "management" issues. This saddened me. First, software engineers should be aware of the legal and ethical implications of their activities, as discussed in the contributions by Liz Duff, Duncan Langford and Dave Pitt (Chapters 4, 2 and 3). Without this knowledge they may be too easily seduced by the technical nature of the software problem and forget its broader implications. Second, it begs the question: if managers only manage and programmers only program then how do programmers recognize good management or prepare themselves for the inevitability of managing?

The sceptic's attitude is probably left over from a time before software engineers — when programmers and analysts existed in isolation. As John Madsen observes in Chapter 7 of this book, in the Dark Ages of computing, computer people were strange and wonderful to behold. They did not conform to business conventions in terms of dress or behaviour. They were mad boffins and therefore forgiven all eccentricities. Indeed, they were expected to be weird. Some of these expectations are still with us, the software professional is still viewed as different from other professionals. However, we increasingly have to work in teams, deal with clients and demonstrate that we can behave responsibly, that is, in a professional manner, according to a professional code of conduct. If this involves dressing for the part, remember that a computer can't wear a suit!

About the author

Colin Myers used to be a practising software engineer, but is now a principal lecturer at the University of Westminster. Concerning the actual worth of suits and wearing them, the following quote from [Wittgenstein, 1966] epitomizes his ambivalence:

> What does a person who knows a good suit say when trying on a suit at the tailor's? "That's the right length", "That's too short', "That's too narrow". Words of approval play no role, although he will look pleased when the coat suits him. Instead of "That's too short" I might say "Look!" or instead of "Right" I might say "Leave it as it is." A good cutter may not use any words at all, but just make a chalk mark and later alter it. How do I show approval of a suit? Chiefly by wearing it often, liking it when it is seen, etc.
>
> You could regard the rules laid down for the measurement of a coat as an expression of what certain people want. People separate on the point of what a coat should measure: there were some who didn't care if it was broad or narrow, etc.; there were some who cared an enormous lot. The rules of harmony, you can say, expressed the way people wanted chords to follow — their wishes crystallized in these rules (the word wishes is much too vague).

References and further reading

Brautigan R. (1968), *All Watched Over by Machines of Loving Grace*, quoted in [Mowshowitz, 1977].

Brooks F. (1975), *The Mythical Man Month*, Addison-Wesley.

Brown F. (1954), *The Answer*, quoted in [Mowshowitz, 1977].

Carlsson C. with Leger M. (1990), *Bad Attitude: The Processed World Anthology*, Verso.

Checkland P. (1981), *Systems Thinking, Systems Practice*, Wiley.

Checkland P. and Scholes J. (1990), *Soft Systems Methodology in Action*, Wiley.

Douglas M. (ed.) (1973), *Rules and Meanings*, Penguin.

Kidder T. (1983), *The Soul of a New Machine*, Penguin.

Mowshowitz A. (1977), *Inside Information, Computers in Fiction*, Addison-Wesley.

Thimbleby H. (1990), *You're right about the cure: don't do that*, in Interacting with Computers vol 2 no 1, Butterworth.

Wittgenstein L. (1966), *Wittgenstein's Tailor* quoted in [Douglas, 1973].

TWO

ETHICS AND PROFESSIONAL CONDUCT
BY DUNCAN LANGFORD

2.1 Introduction

Most software engineers have heard something about ethics, even if they may think of the subject as irrelevant — an undefined "Arts" concept, which has little to do with them. Even without a generally accepted definition, ethics has become a rather fashionable term. We read of people needing to act in an ethical way; frequently, it seems, there are calls for computer scientists to exercise "ethical responsibility" in their work. Companies have made statements on ethical issues, while the public are understood to demand it — and in recent years new computer-related legislation has certainly reflected a perceived public need for greater professional responsibility.

Whether or not we have given thought to the issue, we are working in an environment in which others are clearly prepared and ready to use the concept of *ethics* to define both what is appropriate for us to do, and how we should do it. If clients, employers and the general public really do have such an agenda, even the most cynical software engineer may feel that giving thought to ethics is a sensible precaution.

This chapter briefly examines what *ethics* may be, and looks at the relevance to a professional software engineer. It addresses practical questions such as, "What does the term 'ethics' actually mean?", and "Where do ethical values come from?", as well as a more immediately practical issue — "Can room for a set of restrictive codes be justified in a software engineer's overloaded tool kit?". Examination of these points suggests the need for possession of a personal view of what is ethical, influenced and supported by a generally recognized and accepted code of conduct. The details of such a professional code are then studied, using the BCS (British Computer Society) Code of Conduct as a specific example. Finally, the main strands of ethical issues are brought together, and conclusions drawn.

2.2 What is ethics?

For our purposes, I would suggest that *ethics* be taken to deal with personal uncertainties and conflicts of opinion: "Which alternative action should I take?", "Is this conduct unfair?", and so on. It is of course possible to step further back, and ask wider queries which attempt to analyse more general positions: "If this action is said to be right, what does 'right' really mean?", and similar issues; but however potentially interesting they may be, such questions must lie outside the scope of this chapter.

It is, however, necessary to distinguish between ethics as crime, and ethics as quality of service. For example, using a position as consultant to gain access to a company in order to steal equipment is unethical as well as illegal. However, the issue of how low to pitch quality of service — "what's the minimum can I get away with?" — is clearly legal, but distinctly dubious ethically.

The concept of ethics is not alien to a software engineer. It may well be that we are already operating under a scheme of values which could be re-labelled as ethical, once definitions are clearer. For example, reacting to a new professional situation normally involves reference to a previously relevant experience, or reference to a higher authority, or both. If these responses allow the views of an individual to be formalized and codified, the result takes on the attributes of an ethical code, even where there has been no conscious analysis involved in the formalization process.

A simple instance of such a rule is: "I will not present someone else's code as mine". The decision will probably have been unconsciously developed over a period of time. This may have been through observation of the consequences on someone who did, or the result of teaching, in school, home or church; or it may have been the result of simple expediency. Whatever route was taken, the process of adding rules such as this to others in a personal "experience pack" is usually informal.

If it contains similar rules and guidelines, does a such personal experience-pack amount to a set of ethical standards? Generally, no; there is at least one essential difference between an *ad hoc* set of experience-based rules and an ethical code. It lies in an indispensable filtering stage — a degree of considered analysis. In this assessment, the individual tests each potential addition to their list of ethical views to find whether or not it is genuinely suitable. A typical question might be "Am I prepared to accept this concept as appropriate for me? If I do, what are the implications?". It is this *personal* examination and testing of beliefs which has the potential to transform an unconsidered, pragmatic scheme of values into an individual ethical code.

Of course, there are focused external opinions which, after evaluating, may be incorporated, too. As will be discussed later, the deliberate integration of a professional Code of Practice can enlarge and reinforce a personal internal code; but, however well written, it must be tested in the same way. Unless personally accepted, a global Code of Practice can never replace a personal ethical code.

It is important to stress that although such a personally developed code must be able to evolve and grow, it cannot be constantly redefined and changed, and needs to remain in balance. What is perceived by an individual as unethical behaviour on one day should, reasonably, still be seen by them as unethical behaviour the next.

For our purposes *ethics* will be taken to refer to a particular personal code of conduct. It may be integrated with appropriate external standards, such as an official code of professional practice, and potentially also collated from a variety of other external sources. Whatever the source material, an ethical code ends with an essential process of conscious deliberation, which directly addresses the relevance of the code to an individual's beliefs. This is an essential stage: however well recommended, items which cannot be integrated with personal beliefs must be rejected.

Possession of such a personal ethical code can directly assist individuals in determining how to react to potentially challenging new situations.

2.3 Why be ethical?

> Raj was a consultant evaluating a company's computer system. Raj discovered by accident that several users were storing numbers of strongly pornographic digital images. Although clear about the undesirability, Raj didn't know whether to advise action on moral grounds, or to obscure the real issue behind a much more acceptable issue of disk quotas.

There are both personal and professional components of an ethical code;

"how I behave" is obviously influenced by "who I am" and "where I come from", as well as by the task I am currently employed to do. The professional relevance of an ethical code will be discussed in the next section, but, as development of a personal code of ethics has, by definition, to be personal, it is appropriate to first look at the personal advantages of an ethical code. Clearly, it is impossible to provide universally acceptable reasons for any particular individual to be personally ethical. I'd therefore suggest that, before deciding whether a particular ethical view is appropriate, you spend time in thinking through your own motivations.

In discussions of ethical issues with computer science undergraduates, three particular incentives have regularly been perceived by them as personally relevant; these points may be personally important to you, too:

1. **Trust**
   An individual known to operate under a consistent code of personal ethics is one who can be relied upon.
2. **Security**
   Being aware of the consequences of your actions can guard against unexpected outcomes.
3. **Comfort**
   This is admittedly subjective — but peace of mind may be the most important benefit of all.

2.4 What relevance has ethics to a software engineer?

Software engineers usually work either with or within companies, and must normally consider the wider commercial picture in addition to their own narrow area. Generally, of course, the problems faced in almost any business-oriented profession are not unique to a particular country, or even to a particular continent, while what is culturally acceptable in one part of the world may not be so in another. Increasingly, the move to global business has resulted in the introduction of new business practices — perhaps familiar in one setting, but creating potential problems when imposed on others.

Formal company rules and regulations are probably less important than their unwritten rules — after all, it is at least possible in theory to study a company's official rulebook before taking up an offer of employment. Informal workplace expectations are often much less obvious. As a simple example, the unspoken philosophy of a workaholic start-up company will expect fourteen-hour days from its staff, and be at odds with the needs of some of those staff for a family life. The important, unwritten expectations companies make on employees clearly vary — and not only in the sphere of working hours.

> Lee was newly employed by a medium sized software house, and was placed immediately on a project team. Expecting to write original code, to Lee the deadlines given by the line manager appeared unrealistically severe. Lee soon learnt that, partly to qualify for productivity bonuses, the new team made an unofficial practice of 'borrowing' code from other teams' projects, code often already charged to previous customers.

When does an "unreasonable" expectation become "unacceptable"? If, for Lee, this was such an instance, could Lee have been helped in judging it, and deciding what to do? Perhaps, if before facing this situation, Lee had already thought through the limits of what was believed to be appropriate professional behaviour, and had resource to the support of an accepted, comprehensive professional code ...?

> A computer science student applied to work for a software company as a summer job. Its managing director (it was a small company) made crystal clear at the interview a belief that the reputation of the firm for ethical behaviour was central to its success. The student mentioned, as an example, two competing companies continuing to use their services, each confident that commercial secrets would not be compromised.

Of course, a reputation for cutting costs by cutting corners might work in the short term — but how many clients, given the chance, would actually prefer to take the services of a company of dubious ethical standards? Could an ethical company be formed from a combination of individuals who do not themselves have their own ethical codes?

On a smaller scale, the same rules apply within companies. If, as a team leader, you are given the task of selecting a new member of your team, what qualities would you feel appropriate? I'd suggest good professional practice really should be on the list somewhere!

Let me conclude this section by summarizing its main point. Because it is not cost effective — or, generally, even possible — for client or customer to double check every line of code, some measure of trust in the software engineer's professional competence is essential. Someone who is known to be ethical can be trusted and relied upon in a way that others cannot; a company known to be practising ethical work may enjoy similar confidence.

2.5 Professional codes

Although personal in application, professional codes of conduct can be viewed as the formal expression by professional organizations of the expectations and requirements they make of their members. Indeed, one of the definitions of a profession is that it provides regulation of its members. It is important to stress that this does not mean the contents of a code are only of relevance to members of the organization which drew it up. Whether or not they are members of the organization, everyone working in the relevant field needs to be aware of what is considered appropriate behaviour, and has a legitimate interest in knowing of attempts to define it. Individuals who are not members of professional bodies may well incorporate all or part of the "official" code into their personal ethical standards.

To summarize, important reasons why professional codes of conduct exist are:

1. To allow those within and outside a profession — including the general public — to evaluate exactly what should be expected from members of that profession.
2. To provide clear definitions of what is — and is not — acceptable professional behaviour.

The coherent expression of such an "official" view of professional behaviour has several real advantages. There are personal ones — for example, as mentioned earlier, setting out a detailed written code makes it much easier for an individual to understand the range of circumstances that might be met in their professional life. Such planning is not only to do with uncommon problems — far from it. Some situations may be extremely common: but that need not mean they are consequently unimportant. A comprehensive range of events, beyond the scope of even a well-informed individual, might need to be anticipated if a professional is to feel secure. With the demands of modern business, for instance, it is all too easy to lose sight of wider perspectives under the barrage of day-to-day pressures. The nature of specialization is also inherently likely to obscure the more extended implications of professional actions.

On an industry-wide scale, codes of conduct allow the greater weight of collective views to be felt — the general public may be reassured that those working within a field are also concerned with its standards.

Closer to home, individual commercial decisions by clients and customers can undoubtedly be favourably influenced by the confidence inherent in a well-publicized professional code. Put simply, this is analogous to the establishment of international software standards. Proper compliance with such standards can be advertised and depended upon, so that whoever actually supplies the software and wherever in the world they are located, customers can be sure of what they are buying.

In order to become a member of a professional assocation, an individual is expected to demonstrate high standards of technical competence. If, as a condition of membership, all members of a professional organization subscribe to the same code of conduct, then potential customers and employers can be assured, without further enquiry, of high standards in both skill and behaviour.

Collective expression, of what is believed to be appropriate behaviour for members, is at the core of a professional association. It is important to emphasize that behaviour defined by the professional body as inappropriate, even if it may be legal, is not permitted. All members of a profession are therefore constrained in their behaviour by accepting the limits of the code; but, even for the sceptical, the resultant professional benefits should be obvious.

2.6 Personal versus professional issues

Before examining an example of a professional code, it is appropriate to distinguish between two very different ways of responding to the issues outlined above.

Traditionally, professionals have grouped together into professional bodies, which have then acted as arbiters of behaviour — in the UK, the BMA (British Medical Association) and the Law Society are two long-standing examples. With changes in society and the advent of new technologies, other professional associations have been formed; one is discussed below. However, there are alternatives to viewing professional practice as something to be fixed and regulated from above.

Richard Stallman, inventor of the original EMACS editor, is an example of a rather more personal attempt to define what is appropriate professional behaviour for a software engineer. He has written a complete, UNIX compatible software system called GNU (standing for "Gnu's Not UNIX") with the intention of giving it away. He has presented his philosophy in the aptly-named GnuManifesto, which, although not updated since 1985, is still well worth reading. Here is an extract which probably sums up Stallman's philosophy:†

> Many programmers are unhappy about the commercialization of system software. It may enable them to make more money, but it requires

† Available by anonymous ftp from labrea.stanford.edu in the directory /pub/gnu/GNUinfo or from svin02.info.win.tue.nl in the directory /pub/gnu/GNUinfo.

them to feel in conflict with other programmers in general rather than feel as comrades. The fundamental act of friendship among programmers is the sharing of programs; marketing arrangements now typically used essentially forbid programmers to treat others as friends. The purchaser of software must choose between friendship and obeying the law. Naturally, many decide that friendship is more important. But those who believe in law often do not feel at ease with either choice. They become cynical and think that programming is just a way of making money.

By working on and using GNU rather than proprietary programs, we can be hospitable to everyone and obey the law. In addition, GNU serves as an example to inspire and a banner to rally others to join us in sharing. This can give us a feeling of harmony which is impossible if we use software that is not free. For about half the programmers I talk to, this is an important happiness that money cannot replace.

Although most of us may not be able or even wish to follow such ideas to their limits, knowledge of alternative views is important. Even a convinced supporter of professionalism needs to make an informed choice.

2.7 The BCS Code of Practice

The British Computer Society (the Society of Information Systems Engineering) was established by Royal Charter in 1984 in order to represent professional computer scientists in the UK.

The BCS has placed considerable importance on professional skills and responsibilities, and, after consultation within and beyond the Information Systems field, in 1992 the Society's Professional Advisory Committee recommended a new and comprehensive Professional Code of Practice. This Code sets out the views of the BCS on all aspects of professional practice, and is binding upon BCS members.

A solid knowledge of the BCS Code is essential to any UK practitioner in the field of software engineering, whether or not they are or intend to be members of the BCS. The Code is also of wider relevance, although practitioners in the USA should certainly also consider it in association with the ACM's (Association for Computing Machinery) Code of Ethics and Professional Conduct.

Although the BCS Code of Practice is the definitive document, the BCS pamphlet *British Computer Society Code of Conduct* covers the same ground and is certainly more readable. (It is reproduced in full as Appendix 2A.) Rather than the complex series of Level One (brief, defining statements) and Level Two (supportive rationale for each statement) of the Code of Practice, the pamphlet sets out the essentials by grouping its central points under four main headings:

1. The public interest
2. Duty to employers and clients
3. Duty to the profession
4. Professional competence and integrity

These headings indicate the broad scale and wide scope of the Code. Each section contains a number of specific points and, although for reasons of space it is not possible to deal with the complete contents in detail here, it is important to provide at least a "flavour" of the Code, by discussing examples of points from each heading in turn.

2.7.1 The public interest

The BCS places considerable importance on protection of the public. Rights of third parties must be regarded and respected. However, the Code additionally looks to wider issues. Public health, safety and concern for the environment are all addressed, while an important clause directly emphasizes the need for computer scientists to have regard for basic human rights.

These issues may not usually be at the forefront of a software engineer's mind; nevertheless they are of crucial importance. The designers of computer systems may, through their work, influence the lives of only a few people or of many others, perhaps including those they have never met or even seen. Our world is made from the consequences of professional decisions; and it is perhaps too easy to leave for others' consideration the wider effects of our work. Regrettably, "I'm just concerned with the software. It's not my responsibility" is not an unusual response. However, our software is our responsibility; and we need to be aware of this even if we are not BCS members.

The ACM Code, reproduced as Appendix 2B, is divided into just four main headings, and covers much the same ground. Interestingly, this area is described there under "General Moral Imperatives".

2.7.2 Duty to employers and clients

It is surely axiomatic that clients should be able to trust professional advice. Even if you do not believe computing should be viewed as a profession, this should surely be true. For instance, if you pay a consultant to advise you on the best commercial accounting system for your needs then you have a right to expect an objective response, rather than a salesman's automatic advice to buy a package from their company. It is only reasonable to expect that any professional will be in a position to advise their clients objectively — they should not, for example, use the request for advice as an opportunity to promote a system in which they have a financial interest.

Of course, occasions will arise when a consultant objectively feels their own product is indeed the best choice. In this case, they must make a full disclosure of their involvement to the client before making their recommendation. The same action is essential, for example, where a commission is payable from a third party — the client needs to know of it before making a decision.

The same approach is relevant when working within a company. An employer naturally expects a software engineer to perform work to an agreed standard. If, without agreement, an engineer instead applies an alternative design principally to increase overtime pay, they are almost certainly acting unethically.

Confidentiality is also important, in a world where data held on computers may well be valuable or sensitive or both. It can easily happen, in the course of professional work, that a software engineer becomes aware of information which is confidential. This is not at all uncommon — it could be argued, for example, that the designer or maintainer of a database has fuller access than do any of its likely users. However, access to information does not convey freedom to distribute it. The BCS Code makes it clear that information gained through professional duties should never be disclosed (unless by the consent of the client or by court order).

Another area of potential difficulty lies in making clients aware of the limitations of professional work as well as its advantages. Of course, completion of work should always be to time, and to budget. In real life, though, this condition may sometimes prove difficult to achieve. If a realistic assessment shows that — for instance — an overrun is likely, the ethical software engineer should make their customer aware of the possibility, in good time. Any foreseeable consequences also need to be explained.

There is nothing dramatic or remarkable about the actions expected by this section — common sense should indicate the appropriate ethical choice. A software engineer who lies about deadlines, takes advantage of confidential information from clients and makes recommendations on the basis of personal profit is clearly not someone to employ.

Why, then, is it worth detailing the points? Not just to make the ground rules clear, important as that is. It is also a good example of advantages that membership of organizations like the BCS can bring. In a world where unreliable software engineers exist, making new customers and clients aware that you follow the BCS Code could be a sensible means of establishing goodwill.

2.7.3 Duty to the profession

Belonging to a professional body does not simply mean taking from it what you need in the way of status and support. Membership also brings responsibilities. The BCS expects members will seek to uphold its reputation, both by avoiding actions which could bring it into disrepute, and by working to positively improve the public image of the profession. Members are expected to look for false and misleading statements about their profession, in order to counter them.

It is arguable that this responsibility should also be carried by those outside the BCS — the profession as a whole. As software engineers, we all carry a similar responsibility to ensure our profession is well regarded, and we stand to benefit when it is.

Because of the need to convey a positive image of the profession, BCS members should not make any public statement in their professional capacity unless they are both properly qualified and authorized to do so.

2.7.4 Professional competence and integrity

The final section of the Code addresses the tricky area of professional competence.

A key point to establish here is that membership of a professional body is not the end of a development process. To obtain membership and afterwards take no further efforts — particularly to upgrade relevant knowledge — is held to be insufficient. Particularly in a fast moving discipline, it is essential to keep in touch with both technological developments and altering standards. To do this is not only reassuring to clients but of real importance in personal and professional development.

Self-knowledge, of individual abilities and competence, is also important. This of course means you need to be aware of what you are able to accomplish professionally; but just as important is to know what you cannot do. Despite obvious short-term advantages, it is both unethical and unprofessional to accept work for which are not qualified. Any professional opinion you give, for example, should not only be objective but also be well-founded.

Final points in this section cover more general aspects of "professional" behaviour, common to most professions — not dropping a contract without proper notice, avoiding conflicts of interest, working to good, accepted standards and encouraging subordinates to do so, too. It is important to appreciate that these generally expected standards, common to other professions, are as much part of the Code as are standards unique to computing.

2.7.5 Summary of the Code

If individuals are to build an effective ethical code then they must draw upon a range of ideas and experiences. The BCS Code has the advantage of bringing together a large number of the ethical issues which will confront anyone in professional practice as a software engineer, and presenting guidelines and responses to them which are widely believed to be appropriate. Of course, membership of the BCS automatically (and properly) brings with it a commitment to honour all points in the Code.

Important as the points covered in it are, I do not suggest that this — or any — Code should ever be followed unthinkingly or incorporated into a personal set of beliefs without question. Codes are not set in stone and should never be thought of as a substitute for individual thought. In this case, the profession as well as the individual is developing, and it is important that the Code is kept under review. It is, of course, for BCS members to help in its evolution.

2.8 Conclusions

In this chapter I have stressed the personal and professional importance to a professional software engineer of being aware of the results of their actions, and of the need of each individual to possess their own ethical code of behaviour. There is need also to appreciate the relationship between a professional action and the code which governs it. Professional development depends upon effective knowledge of accepted standards of professional practice and behaviour.

Particularly in a fast moving field such as computing, the limitations of yesterday are unlikely to remain unchanged. New areas of computer-related ethical problems seem to develop with bewildering rapidity, and a code which was comprehensive when written is likely to need constant revision to keep pace with developing technology. For example, the rapid spread of virtual reality systems is largely untouched by present codes. Is it appropriate for a software engineer to assist in development of a virtual reality system without giving attention to the potential effects it could have on users? Or to employ imaging techniques reliant on lasers drawing directly onto the eye? Or to design a computer game intended to be addictive?

Whatever the current state of technological development, the work of individual software engineers will always be at the forefront. It is for them to confront the issues discussed in this chapter, and others as yet unknown; and for them to match their actions to their ethical beliefs.

There are no easy options — but the most difficult option of all is to pretend the issues do not exist.

About the author

Dr Duncan Langford was a late entry to the computing field, first qualifying as a social worker, and spending fifteen years in local authority social services. He eventually resigned to gain postgraduate degrees in computing, and now teaches computing — and ethics — at the Computing Laboratory of the University of Kent, Canterbury.

He has, of course, seen a suit and understands their use in theory; but his lack of first-hand knowledge is depressingly obvious to the most casual observer.

Further reading

Anderson E., Johnson D., Gotterbarn D. and Perrolle J. (1993), *Using the New ACM Code of Ethics*, Communications of the ACM, vol 36, no 1, February 1993.

Bynum T., Maner W. and Fodor J. (eds) (1991), *Teaching computer ethics* in *Proceedings of the 'Teaching computing and human values' National Conference on Computing and Values, 1991*, Southern Connecticut State University, Research Center on Computing and Society.

Collins R. *et al.* (1994), *How Good is Good Enough? An Ethical Analysis of Software Construction and Use*, Communications of the ACM, vol 37, no 1, January 1994.

Dejoie R., Fowler G. and Paradice D. (eds) (1991), *Ethical Issues in Information Systems*, Boyd and Fraser.

Ermann M., Williams M. and Gutierrez C. (eds) (1990), *Computers, Ethics and Society*, Oxford University Press.

Forester T. and Morrison P. (1990), *Computer ethics: cautionary tales and ethical dilemmas in computing*, Blackwells.

Johnson D. (1985), *Computer Ethics*, Prentice-Hall.

Langford D. (1995), *Practical Computer Ethics*, McGraw-Hill.

Mackie J. (1990), *Ethics: Inventing Right and Wrong*, Penguin.

Parker D., Swope S. and Baker B. (1990), *Ethical Conflicts in Information and Computer Science, Technology and Business*, QED Inc.

APPENDIX 2A   BCS RULES OF PROFESSIONAL CONDUCT

As an aid to understanding, these rules have been grouped in the principal duties which all members should endeavour to discharge in pursuing their professional lives.†

The public interest

1. Members shall in their professional practice safeguard public health and safety and have regard to the protection of the environment.
2. Members shall have due regard to the legitimate rights of third parties.
3. Members shall ensure that within their chosen fields they have knowledge and understanding of relevant legislation, regulations and standards and that they comply with such requirements.
4. Members shall in their professional practice have regard to basic human rights and shall avoid any actions that adversely affect such rights.

Duty to employers and clients

5. Members shall carry out work with due care and diligence in accordance with the requirements of the employer or client and shall, if their professional judgement is overruled, indicate the likely consequences.
6. Members shall endeavour to complete work undertaken on time and to budget and shall advise their employer or client as soon as practicable if any overrun is foreseen.
7. Members shall not offer or provide, or receive in return, any inducement for the introduction of business from a client unless there is full prior disclosure of the facts to that client.
8. Members shall not disclose or authorize to be disclosed, or use for personal gain or to benefit a third party, confidential information acquired in the course of professional practice, except with prior written permission of the employer or client or at the direction of a court of law.
9. Members should seek to avoid being put in a position where they may become privy to or party to activities or information concern-

† © 1992 BCS. Reproduced by permission.

ing activities which would conflict with their responsibilities in 1-4 above.

10. Members should not misrepresent or withhold information on the capabilities of products, systems or services with which they are concerned or take advantage of the lack of knowledge or inexperience of others.
11. Members shall not, except where specifically so instructed, handle client's monies or place contracts or orders in connection with work on which they knowingly have any interest, financial or otherwise.
12. Members shall not purport to exercise independent judgement on behalf of a client on any product or service which they knowingly have any interest, financial or otherwise.

Duty to the profession

13. Members shall uphold the reputation of the Profession and shall seek to improve professional standards through participation in their development, use and enforcement, and shall avoid any action which will adversely affect the good standing of the Profession.
14. Members shall in their professional practice seek to advance public knowledge and understanding of computing and information systems and technology and to counter false or misleading statements which are detrimental to the Profession.
15. Members shall encourage and support fellow members in their professional development and, where possible, provide opportunities for the professional development of new entrants to the Profession.
16. Members shall act with integrity towards fellow members and to members of other professions with whom they are concerned in a professional capacity and shall avoid engaging in any activity which is incompatible with professional status.
17. Members shall not make any public statement in their professional capacity unless properly qualified and, where appropriate, authorized to do so, and shall have due regard to the likely consequences of any such statement on others.

Professional competence and integrity

18. Members shall seek to upgrade their professional knowledge and skill and shall maintain awareness of technological developments, procedures and standards which are relevant to their field, and shall encourage their subordinates to do likewise.
19. Members shall seek to conform to recognized good practice including quality standards which are in their judgement relevant, and shall encourage their subordinates to do likewise.

20. Members shall only offer to do work or provide service which is within their professional competence and shall not lay claim to any level of competence which they do not posses, and any professional opinion which they are asked to give shall be objective and reliable.
21. Members shall accept professional responsibility for their work and for the work of subordinates and associates under their direction, and shall not terminate any assignment except for good reason and on reasonable notice.
22. Members shall avoid any situation that may give rise to a conflict of interest between themselves and their client and shall make full and immediate disclosure to the client if any such conflict should occur.

APPENDIX 2B   THE ACM CODE OF ETHICS AND PROFESSIONAL CONDUCT

The following is a summary of the ACM (Association of Computing Machinery) code of ethics and professional conduct as adopted by the ACM Council in October 1992.†

General moral imperatives

As an ACM member I will

1. Contribute to society and human well-being
2. Avoid harm to others
3. Be honest and trustworthy
4. Be fair and take action not to discriminate
5. Honor property rights including copyrights and patents
6. Give proper credit for intellectual property
7. Respect the privacy of others
8. Honor confidentiality

More specific professional responsibilities

As an ACM computing professional, I will

1. Strive to achieve the highest quality, effectiveness, and dignity in both the process and products of professional work.

† © 1992 ACM. Reproduced by permission.

2. Acquire and maintain professional competence.
3. Know and respect existing laws pertaining to professional work.
4. Accept and provide appropriate professional review.
5. Give comprehensive and thorough evaluations of computer systems and their impacts, including analysis of possible risks.
6. Honor contracts, agreements, and assigned responsibilities.
7. Improve public understanding of computing and its consequences.
8. Access computing and communication resources only when authorized to do so.

Organizational leadership imperatives

As an ACM member and an organizational leader, I will

1. Articulate social responsibilities of members of an organizational unit and encourage full acceptance of those responsibilities.
2. Manage personnel and resources to design and build information systems that enhance the quality of working life.
3. Acknowledge and support proper and authorized uses of an organization's computing and communication resources.
4. Ensure that users and those who will be affected by a system have their needs clearly articulated during the assessment and design of requirements; later, the system must be validated to meet [its] requirements.
5. Articulate and support policies that protect the dignity of users and others affected by a computing system.
6. Create opportunities for members of the organization to learn the principles and limitations of computer systems.

Compliance with the Code

As an ACM member, I will

1. Uphold and promote the principles of this code.
2. Treat violations of this code as inconsistent with membership in the ACM.

THREE

IMPLICATIONS OF THE DATA PROTECTION ACT

BY DAVE PITT

3.1 Introduction

Ever since the Data Protection Act came into force in the UK in 1984, it has had many detractors. It has been criticized by some as a piece of unnecessary bureaucracy, slowing up the workings of the Free Market, by others as a sop to foil the demand for a truly effective Act. In this chapter, I will examine the effectiveness of the Act and show what value it has for the software engineer.

This chapter will begin with an overview of the terms of the Act. Then I will discuss the implications of the Act, and finally discuss some ways of improving it. I will not go into the legal minutiae of the Act: that is done adequately in a number of other texts (see the Further reading at the end of this chapter). The goal here is to look at the Act from the viewpoint of a software engineer, not a corporate lawyer.

3.2 The Principles of the Data Protection Act

The Data Protection Act is essentially a mechanism for enforcing eight Data Protection Principles. These Principles are legally binding, that is, they are not a Code of Conduct which you are advised, but not obliged, to follow; they have the force of law, and if you ignore them, the consequences can be serious.

The eight Principles are concerned with the correct use of "personal data" held on computer, personal data being defined as any data from which an individual person may be identified. The Principles state that personal data must be:

1. **Obtained and processed fairly and lawfully.**

   Broadly speaking, if personal data is obtained and processed for a purpose for which the organization is registered under the Act, this Principle will be met. Realization of this has caused much dissatisfaction amongst the public, who thought that one of the purposes of the Act was to outlaw certain categories of data (perhaps the grosser forms of computerized junk mail, and so on). The Act does nothing of the kind; in effect, all it says is: "Thou shalt use data only for uses for which you have registered."

2. **Held for specified purposes.**

   A specified purpose is one which an organization has declared in its registration. A competent registration, which covers in broad terms the scope of an organization's activities, is enough to meet this obligation. Again, the public have a understandable sense of betrayal at the weakness of this Principle.

3. **Not disclosed for any other, incompatible purpose.**

   This Principle more or less repeats Principle 2 in a negative sort of way. It says that if an organization holds data for one purpose, it must not also hold it for a contradictory purpose. Indeed!

4. **Adequate, relevant and not excessive.**

   Depending how this Principle is interpreted, this is potentially one of the most useful requirements of the Act since it strikes at the tendency for computer systems to amass more and more data about people.

5. **Accurate and up to date.**

   Again, potentially a very useful Principle, because more and more important decisions about individuals (their job-worthiness, their credit-worthiness, to name but two) are made on the basis of computer records, and these are notoriously inaccurate. Inaccuracy which leads to a data subject suffering damage may entitle that individual to compensation.

6. **Held for no longer than necessary.**

   An excellent Principle to have, but its practical usefulness depends on the definition of how long is "necessary" — generally, a Court would accept whatever is the norm for the industry.
   and . . .

7. **An individual must be entitled (at reasonable intervals, without undue cost or delay) to know whether any information is held about him or her, have a right to access it, and correct or delete it as appropriate.**

   More than any other, this is the key Principle of the Act, since it establishes the right of individuals to know what an organization has on file about them. It is limited both by a number of exemptions and exclusions, and by certain structural weaknesses which I will describe later on, but potentially this Principle is a considerable advance for the rights of the individual in the UK.

8. **Appropriate security measures must be taken.**

   Appropriate security measures must be taken against unauthorized access to, alteration, disclosure or destruction of personal data.

3.2.1 Exceptions and exclusions

There are some qualifications to the Principles, the most important being:

1. **The Act applies to computerized records only.**

   It is a paranoid organization which opts to keep its data on paper and forgo the benefits of computerization rather than fall within the scope of the Act. Of more practical interest, word-processing is exempted from the Act, the rationale being that word-processing is a glorified form of typing and, as such, not really data processing.

2. **Records associated with national security are excluded.**

   Such exemptions are defined by a Cabinet Minister or the Attorney General. It sometimes stretches credibility what is categorized as national security — whole swathes of the work of the armed forces, the Ministry of Defence, the Home Office, and so on.

3. **Records associated with payroll and accounts are excluded.**

   Records which are specifically for these limited purposes are exempt.

4. **Records associated with crime, taxation etc. are excluded.**

   This applies wherever personal data is held for the detection or prevention of crime — the police do not have to disclose their information to a suspect. Similarly the taxation authorities do not have to disclose their tax records.

5. **Records of a purely domestic or other similar nature are excluded.**

   There are three cases where this exemption applies:
   ◇ Domestic purposes, such as personal financial records held on a personal computer.
   ◇ The records of small, unincorporated, clubs — the school chess club, say.
   ◇ Mailing lists for such domestic purposes.

6. **Records about the dead are excluded.**
7. **Records which state intentions, as opposed to facts or opinions, are excluded.**
   This is a strange exemption, since *I intend to fire Joe* (an intention) and *Joe ought to be fired* (an opinion) and *Joe will be fired* (a fact) all mean more or less the same thing. However, this is chiefly of interest to the lawyers amongst us since no real-life organization is going to rewrite its records to take advantage of this loophole.
8. **Medical or social work records are excluded.**
   The argument here is that the public should not have a right to see their own medical and other such records without the guidance and permission of a professional in case they misinterpret the information therein.
9. **Statistical or research data, or exam marks are excluded.**
   Suppose an Aids researcher holds case histories about individual Aids patients. Since the individual element is incidental to the research, it is reasonable that it should remain secret. Similarly, it is reasonable to keep exam marks confidential until they can be properly announced.

These are the main exemptions; there are a number of others for which you may consult the legal textbooks. If this list seems to give scope for avoiding registration, you should realize that the exclusions are only designed to filter out items of a purely domestic nature, items sensitive to the Government or its agencies, or items such as medical records which need to be interpreted by an expert, and various other things irrelevant to the main thrust of the Act. Everything else will be within the scope of the Act, and practically every organization, however humble, will need to register under the Act.

3.2.2 Registration and other formalities

The mechanics of registration are, in principle, straightforward. To register, you obtain a registration form from the Registrar's office, from Her Majesty's Stationery Office, or from a central library. The form asks you to register all categories of personal data your organization holds or processes and the uses to which it is put. As there is no penalty or additional cost for ticking too many registration categories, but it is illegal to do things you have not ticked, I recommend you tick every category which could in any way reasonably apply to your organization. You then send off the form with the appropriate fee and your registration is automatically accepted.

However, because there are numerous categories of "Data Subject", "Classes of Data Held", "Sources of Data", "Standard Purpose Titles",

"Countries or Territories to which the Data may be transferred", and so on, it can take a large organization literally weeks of work to collect the required data and fill in the registration form accurately.

When the Act was first instituted, it was the vogue in major companies to appoint full-time Data Protection Administrators. In these cost-conscious times, such luxuries are no longer afforded, and organizations will typically ask a senior person in the legal, administration or computer departments to complete the registration on the basis of their existing knowledge, and to keep a watching brief over re-registration, compliance with the Act, changes to the legislation and so on as a part-time or spare-time activity.

At central libraries, members of the public can inspect your registration, that is, the categories of personal data in which you profess to deal. Upon payment of a fee, which will not exceed £10 (at the time of writing) for each enquiry, they can demand you supply in a reasonable time, and certainly within forty days, a statement describing all the data your organization holds about them on computer for the categories in question.

If the information that you supply conflicts with any of the Principles, for example it is inaccurate or has been wrongfully obtained, then the enquirer can demand the wrong or wrongfully obtained data be removed. Curiously, they cannot demand that you change the wrong data to right data.

The Data Protection Registrar is responsible for the enforcement of the Act. For example, the Registrar monitors non-registration by organizations and threatens or prosecutes them accordingly, issues guidelines to impose particular interpretations of the Act, and investigates individual organizations which may be breaking the Principles.

For non-compliance with the Act, the Registrar can issue:

1. An enforcement notice: this will state the cause of complaint, the steps to be taken to rectify the situation, and how quickly it must be done.
2. A transfer prohibition notice, to prohibit personal data from going overseas.
3. A de-registration notice, which in effect causes the organization to cease trading.

Additionally, an organization can be fined up to £2000 for non-registration in a magistrates' court or an unlimited fine in a higher court.

In practice, these legal powers have been used very sparingly, and it is clear from the level of non-registrations that many organizations consider the likelihood of being prosecuted to be a chance worth taking. However, this is an approach which I cannot recommend — a software engineer should support best industry practice, and taking a chance on registration is not part of this.

3.3 How the Act works

3.3.1 How is it *meant* to work?

Any legislation, however complicated, has at its heart a simple dream, a motivating force, which sustains its supporters through the long days of drafting its clauses, pushing it through Parliament, and defending it thereafter. The Data Protection Act is no exception: its supporters undoubtedly had in mind a scenario like the following:

> An individual is, say, refused credit; they cannot understand this because they believe their credit rating should be high. They therefore use the Data Protection Act to find out from the credit rating company what data they hold about them. They find an error that they demand be rectified. For good measure, the Registrar decides to prosecute the company on the grounds, say, that the data in question was inaccurate and out of date. This concentrates wonderfully the minds of the credit rating industry with the result that standards of data protection are raised all round.

For all the thousands of words of the actual legislation, this is what the Act boils down to, and it is a goal which we can all applaud. This illustration also shows the essential naivety of the Act, for it rests on two beliefs:

1. That data about individuals is simple and objective.
2. That individuals will find it easy enough to obtain information from organizations.

In fact neither of these beliefs is true for any but the most straightforward cases.

3.3.2 How *does* it work in practice?

Degree of enforcement

There have been comparatively few prosecutions under the Act. *Computer Weekly* (October 1988) reported:

The DHSS, which expected 200 000 requests a year, received only 270 in the first four months since the Act came into force. The Home Office has had only sixteen. The biggest number of requests was made to the Ministry of Defence — all from past and present staff.

This is partly because the Registrar believes in encouraging, not cajoling, organizations to comply with the Act, partly because there are insufficient Data Protection staff to take a tougher approach. The result is that many organizations either totally ignore the Act (there is a high number of non-registrations — at the end of 1991, there were 170 000 companies registered, while the Registrar believes the number should be around 250 000), or they register but do very little more — they may make someone "responsible" for its implementation within the organization, but this amounts to a token effort.

In their defence, organizations accuse the Act of irrelevance and duplication of work they have already done. They argue that commercial pressures force upon them far higher standards than the Act ever does — they already hold data securely, otherwise their competitors would steal it; they cannot afford to hold information for longer than strictly necessary because storing data is expensive, and so on. There is some truth in this, but generally it is disingenuous — it simply is not true that there is a perfect match between the commercial interest of an organization and the public interest.

So the picture is one of limited acceptance of the Act by organizations. Many ignore it outright, while many of those who do register pay only lip-service to it.

User-friendliness

Is the Act easy for the public to participate in? Would you, if you thought your credit rating were wrong, pay up to £10 to ask a credit rating company what information they held about you? Would you trust their answer? Would you even know which rating company to approach? — credit providers are notoriously protective of their sources. What if several credit rating companies are involved?

A favourite trick is for an organization to split its business into multiple registrations, which makes enquiries even more expensive. According to Duncan Campbell (*Personal Computer World*, October 1988):

> to fully check the Police National Computer would cost £50. To check all Metropolitan Police or Home Office Computers might cost £250. To check every police computer in the country would cost well over £1000.

This exhausting chase is a long way from the original vision that individuals should have a convenient, affordable and simple means of keeping tabs on what Big Brother holds on them. If the chase is too arduous, the public will not bother. This is what is happening with the Data Protection Act.

The Data Protection Register itself is a forbidding document. It lists for each registered organization, the categories of data it is licensed to use and the types of use it may make of these categories. The categories and types of usage are so bland and numerous as to be virtually meaningless.

For all these reasons, the Act has a large credibility gap with the public. This is reflected in the number of times the public uses the Act, which is excessively low.

National security

This excuse is used far beyond what is necessary to protect the State. A couple of examples of this will suffice.

First, an article by Nick Booth in *PCLAN* (June 1992) describes the case of Metropolitan Police DNA Database. This only came to light when a man who had been given a blood sample to eliminate him from a murder enquiry discovered that the data was being used for another purpose. He requested that the data be deleted from the record but was told that this was not possible.

> What the police were doing in the DNA case was building up a DNA database in secret, not telling the people concerned, not telling the public generally and not telling Parliament. There was no control, there were no safeguards, they didn't even tell the individuals concerned. Now that can't be right.

Second, from the previously quoted article by Duncan Campbell:

> The Act is replete with Kafkaesque characteristically British loopholes. For example, it allows government ministers to issue certificates exempting some computers from scrutiny on grounds of "national security". But no such certificates have apparently been issued, since to issue such certificates would presumably reveal to the somnambulant public that MI5, the Secret Services and other UK intelligence agencies were actually using computers to store personal information.

These examples are typical of Government's attitude to the Act, which is that its agencies are, in so many ways, outside the scope of its own law.

Freedom of information and privacy

Much of the really interesting information nowadays is between Government and its subjects, and typically this will not relate to any one individual. In such cases, you will find it very difficult to make use of the Act. Besides, the national security card is played here by the Government at every possible opportunity. The Data Protection Act is nothing like the US Freedom of Information Act, which gives individuals real powers to uncover such information. Indeed, the position in the UK is, if anything, worse than before the Act because organizations can now hide behind it, saying that by giving out the tiny amount of information which the Act requires them to reveal, they have met their obligations. Many commentators agree that the UK is an obsessively secretive society, and the Act has done little to change this.

Surprisingly, for a country so committed to secrecy, individuals in the UK have practically no right to privacy — they can sue a newspaper for an inaccurate story about themselves, but if the story is factually correct, then they have very little come-back, no matter how private the matters discussed are. Presumably this is because the Old Boy network has in the past protected its own perfectly well without need for legal structures. Whatever the reason, the Data Protection Act does little to help — it says that data must be relevant and not excessive, but still organizations collect, largely unhindered, vast databanks of information about us all.

The defence offered by the architects of the Data Protection Act to these criticisms is that the Act was never meant to be either a Freedom of Information Act or a Privacy Act. Granted, but the Act often fails to deliver even within its own limited terms of reference; and it fails for two reasons:

1. Lack of willingness to prosecute offenders.
2. Lack of clear definitions of terms such as "excessive" or "relevant". Without these terms being properly defined and enforced, organizations will continue to ride roughshod over the Act and over the individual.

3.4 Implications for the software engineer

So far this chapter has been critical of the Data Protection Act. But even if we criticize the Act, we have to deal with it as it stands. It is the "Law of the Land", and it represents a foundation upon which greater things may be built in future. The Data Protection Act, for all its failings, is a necessary and useful piece of legislation.

Moreover, by using the Act as a guide to designing your own systems, you will undoubtedly build better systems. For many reasons, therefore, you would do well to pay attention to it.

So how should software engineers ensure they meet its requirements? The following is a check-list of do's and don'ts.

3.4.1 Registration

As said earlier, be sure your organization is registered. If you do not register, you may well escape prosecution, but:

◇ The consequences can be tough if your organization is prosecuted.
◇ As a responsible software engineer, you should promote the best practices of your profession, which means supporting the Act.

3.4.2 Exemptions

In general, forget these, and concentrate on meeting the Principles since they represent a code of good practice. Of course, you must be aware of the exemptions in so far as they apply to your profession — for example, not having to divulge examination marks prematurely if you teach — but your overall orientation to the Act should be to work with it, not to avoid it wherever possible.

3.4.3 Systems design

Let us consider each Principle in turn and see how they affect systems design:

Personal data must be obtained fairly and lawfully

It always has been illegal to obtain data unlawfully (sic), but now it is also illegal to obtain it unfairly. The Act is particularly concerned to stamp out deception in the collection and processing of personal data. For example, if you give your name and address to enter a competition, it would be unfair if the promoter then put your name onto a customer/contact list without your permission; this is why raffle tickets often have a box to tick if you do not want your name to be used for sending you, say, promotional material.

As a software engineer, you need to consider whether data collected for one purpose might be used for another. For example, medical data which employees give to the company pension scheme should not be passed onto the personnel department for them to use as a basis for a redundancy program. In these days when systems are so interrelated, this can be a big headache for the software engineer; the solution is to establish very clearly who in the company owns the data in question and to make them responsible (in writing) for any data-sharing. Thereafter, you need to invent ways of informing the individual how their data is used. The tick-box on the raffle ticket described above is one way.

Data shall be held for specified purposes

This means that you must not use data for purposes which your company has not declared in its registration. This emphasizes the importance of identifying all possible data uses, sources and so on in your registration. It is perfectly acceptable to update the registration with new categories, and as your organization changes, this will happen from time to time, but it is obviously convenient to do this task as rarely as possible.

As a software engineer, you should be aware of your organization's registration details so that you do not inadvertently develop something for which it is not registered.

Data shall not be disclosed for other, incompatible purposes

This Principle expands upon Principle 2 by saying that personal data should not be used or disclosed in any manner incompatible with its registered, specified purposes.

This Principle means, for example, that if your employer were a research organization and therefore registered to hold and use personal data for research purposes, you must be careful that confidential information about individuals is not revealed when it was given purely for statistical research.

Data must be adequate, relevant and not excessive

Many of the systems designed by UK Local Authorities to collect the Community Charge tax fell foul of this Principle by asking for an individual taxpayer's previous addresses. While it is useful for a Local Authority to know this information, it is not strictly necessary, since only an individual's current address is absolutely required in order to collect the tax. The Data Protection Registrar therefore demanded that the authorities change their systems accordingly.

It is very easy, when you are designing a system, to make provision to hold all sorts of potentially useful data — in the past this has been an excellent design guideline, because it is easy enough to build in additional fields at the beginning of a system development, but more difficult later on. This remains true even if you modularize your systems design as much as possible. However, in future you must test all the data you intend to use against this Principle. If you are designing a market information system, you may be tempted to hold all sorts of information about individuals' tastes, habits, lifestyles, etc. In doing so, you must consider what is strictly relevant to your organization's legitimate interests and what is institutionalized prurience. Do you really need to record an individual's religion on your personnel database? The trouble with software engineers is that they are too eager to please, and they love building databases; they forget that a list of Catholics in Northern Ireland in the 1980s, or Jews in Nazi Germany could be dangerous in the wrong hands. Instead you may want to take an "incremental software development" approach to systems development, that is, to prototype systems which provide you with what you know is needed, rather than to attempt to cater for all future possibilities.

If you are unsure whether your system should hold or manipulate certain data, you should consult your organization's legal adviser before any implementation begins.

If you are unsure whether your system should hold or manipulate certain data, you should consult your organization's legal adviser before doing any programming.

Data shall be accurate and up to date

Of course, no data is totally accurate and up to date. A rule-of-thumb is that at least 10% of the data in any system is inaccurate at any one time. Fortunately, the Registrar will test any complaints about accuracy and timeliness by a reasonableness criterion. If the system in question has adequate procedures in place to identify and correct false or outdated data, then the Act will be satisfied.

Having said this, most systems pay scant regard to ensuring data is correct — somehow that is considered an "operational" task and not important enough for software engineers to concern themselves with.

Such a cavalier attitude may not be acceptable in future. Consider the matter from the point of view of the individual; if your system continually spells their name wrongly, they will complain about you. The fact that the system is run by an incompetent operations manager may not be an excuse if it has insufficient checks and balances built in. A couple of simple examples:

1. A public utility cannot claim that a £1 million bill to an individual was a clerical mistake, because all financial systems should have validity checking to stop such errors; it would be seen as a fault with the system.
2. A marketing organization should consider deleting records from its distribution lists if the record has been dead (no response from mailshots) for a certain length of time.

Information shall not be held for longer than necessary

Systems should be built from the ground up with suitable data retention policies in mind, and good purge facilities are essential for ensuring data is held for appropriate periods.

One of the annoying things about direct mail is that it can seem impossible to stop such mail for people who ceased to live at an address years ago, and one wonders how the direct mail organizations keep their databases up to date.

As a software engineer, in future you will need to spend less time on clever algorithms to optimize database performance, and far more time inventing ways of validating data, providing lists of questionable data, and so on. At its most basic, this derives from a change in the priorities within the computer industry itself — as hardware performance improves exponentially, we are less concerned with squeezing the last ounce of performance out of the software, and much more concerned with guaranteeing the quality of the data.

An individual must be entitled (at reasonable intervals, without undue cost or delay) to know whether any information is held about him or her, have a right to access it, and correct or delete it as appropriate

This is the requirement which is often the hardest to meet. Large organizations simply do not know what information they hold on an individual, and finding this out can require a whole series of complicated *ad hoc* queries against systems running on mainframes and personal computers, batch and real-time systems, current and historical data.

There are two approaches to this problem. The first is to muddle through when an enquiry is received; this usually works well enough to placate the enquirer. This can be an exhausting effort, although surprisingly the staff of the organization often feel good about themselves because they have moved mountains to satisfy the enquirer. But in general, their systems will be unresponsive to such requests for information. This may not matter too much with respect to the Data Protection Act, when the enquiries may be few and far between, but it may be disastrous in terms of their overall ability to give customer satisfaction.

The second approach is to redesign the systems so that the organization can respond to all customers and enquirers with a full and fast answer. As I will explain later in this chapter, this means a total switch of emphasis from a data-centred to a customer-focused model. The effect of this on systems design is fundamental: it will be necessary to re-model practically all of your organization's systems. In terms of data-modelling techniques, you may be looking to use object-oriented techniques rather than data flow diagrams or entity-relationship modelling.

Appropriate security measures must be taken

For all sorts of reasons — to deter hackers, to avoid costly legal actions, to maintain customer confidence, to protect your organization's intellectual property, and of course to comply with the Data Protection Act — you need to take security very seriously.

This is not the place to describe in detail how you go about building secure systems, but some of the principles you need to follow are:

◇ Security must be at a level appropriate to the importance of the data.
◇ Security involves the total system, not just the computerized part of it: for example, you need to check that there is good quality control over the data brought into the system, that passwords are of a suitable complexity and changed regularly, that printout is disposed of securely and does not blow in the wind down the street, and so on.

Summary of the effect on systems design

The Data Protection Act is based on the twin premisses that organizations have an obligation to look after carefully the data "belonging" to individuals and that individuals must have easy access to "their" data. These premisses have radical implications for how organizations (and software engineers) must regard their customers and the public in general. To date, organizations have had a rather guarded approach to the Act; in public they may welcome it, but in private they have often thought up ways to minimize its impact. This is a negative way of looking at things. If they are really committed to customer-focused ways of doing business (and to stay in business these days they must be customer-focused), both organizations and software engineers must become more enthusiastic about the Data Protection Act.

3.5 The alternatives

Given that both organizations and the public have deep-seated reservations about the Act, what can be done to improve its acceptability? Let's look at the alternatives:

1. Self-regulation.
2. Letting the market rule.
3. Letting the Courts decide.
4. Refining the present system.

3.5.1 Self-regulation

Self-regulation is the fashionable belief that an industry or other entity can be relied on to regulate itself in the best interests of all. There are numerous examples of self-regulation, such as sports ruling bodies like the Football Association or professional bodies like the British Computer Society (BCS) or the Stock Exchange Commission.

The argument for self-regulation is simple — who better than the Football Association to run football or the Society of Motor Traders the motor trade? Who indeed — they have, after all, unparalleled experience of their organization, and they cost less to run than an independent body.

The trouble with self-regulatory bodies is their lack of independence of the industry they spring from. They naturally look after themselves first, their customers next, then anyone else a long way after that. The public interest operates only if it coincides with their own self-interest.

In terms of data protection, a body like the BCS might be called upon to provide self-regulation. The BCS would, no doubt, act in a highly competent manner, but its relation to the computer industry would always be cosy, even incestuous — not good for the BCS, and not good for the public. Objectivity really does require independence.

It is often argued that any lack of objectivity by these self-regulators is outweighed by their expertise and cheapness of operation. Neither argument holds much water. Regarding expertise, the first Data Protection Registrar in fact came from the BCS and was highly respected for knowledge both of the industry and of the public's point of view, which a self-regulator will never totally have. So a well-chosen independent body can be better than self-regulation. Regarding cost, the Registrar is financed partly from registration fees, so the net cost to the public is small. In any case, even if the fees were dispensed with, perhaps the vast computer industry could afford an independent, objective watch-dog.

Thus self-regulation does not appear to be the answer.

3.5.2 Letting the market rule

This says the market for data protection should be allowed to reach its own equilibrium, unfettered by unnecessary baggage such as Data Protection Acts, Registrars and the like.

The argument goes like this. Data protection has a benefit to society, composed of the benefit individuals derive from, say, not having their private lives carelessly exposed by slack data security. Data protection also has a cost, composed, for example, of the cost of building security into the relevant computer systems. There will be a point at which this cost and benefit balances — at its crudest, this will be where an organization feels that providing more computer security will cost more than occasionally having to pay damages to individuals when its security fails. At this point, the supply of data protection will equal its demand, and it will have achieved an equilibrium via market mechanisms, without the need for a data protection bureaucracy.

This argument is fine as far as it goes, but that equilibrium is hardly likely to be fair. In terms of data protection, as we have already seen, it is very difficult and time-consuming for an individual to challenge a large organization. So the data protection market will naturally establish an equilibrium which favours organizations over individuals, and this will not be in the national interest. There is a need to correct this. Hence the need for the Data Protection Act.

3.5.3 Letting the Courts decide

Letting the Courts decide is not so different from letting the market decide, except that here the emphasis is on legal, rather then monetary, processes. In effect, judges would replace the Data Protection Registrar, making case law to interpret whatever legislation was in place.

One problem with this approach is that judges seem to be spectacularly ignorant of anything to do with computers; their chief talent in this area is their consistent ability to reach "surprising" judgements. If ever there were a case for leaving things to the experts, their lordships are it.

The Courts are also expensive. Thereby, they structurally favour the rich — in the present context, large corporations — because the rich can afford to hire the best counsel.

What would probably happen, therefore, would be that the general Courts would perform badly, and the Lord Chancellor would be forced to set up specialist Courts to deal more expertly with data protection, perhaps along the lines of Industrial Tribunals. In other words, the Chancellor would re-invent the Data Protection Act.

3.5.4 Refining the present system

We have rejected self-regulation as inherently self-serving; we have argued that the Free Market would produce an unfair situation unless corrected by legislation; and we have argued that the Courts would lack expertise. So what, if anything, can we do to improve the present system? As we have seen, the Act can be criticized for:

1. Being bureaucratic and user-unfriendly.
2. Allowing Government to play the national security card too easily.
3. Not being a Freedom of Information Act or Privacy Act.

What can be done about these issues?

Reducing the bureaucracy

Why make organizations register? — we do not make organizations register under the Health and Safety at Work Act, or the Race Relations Act, or the Infectious Diseases (Notification) Act, yet they have to abide by these regulations just as closely. Why not just enact the Principles then simply set up an Inspectorate to monitor compliance? — like the Health and Safety Inspectorate.

The time it takes each organization to register and renew the registration, plus the bureaucracy required to process the registrations, is considerable. By removing these tasks, we would remove an irritant to organizations and allow the Registrar to be more focused on their real role of enforcing the legislation. The positive impact of this proposal should not be underestimated.

In terms of cost, why not:

1. Cut the maximum fee for an enquiry under the Act: when the Act was set up, the then Home Secretary, Douglas Hurd, was repeatedly warned by organizations like the National Consumer Council and the National Council for Civil Liberties that to set a charge higher than, say, a nominal £1 would completely frustrate the purpose of the Act. Hurd duly set the fee at £10.

2. Allow a refund of the fee if the enquiry is justified: it is not so much the actual amount involved, it's the principle — why should anyone pay to redress an untruth or other discrepancy about themselves that should never have existed in the first place?

3. Disallow the practice whereby organizations split their registration into many parts thus making an enquiry more difficult and costly — a comprehensive check of data held by the Automobile Association, one of the largest direct mailers, would cost you £260. On the other hand, British Rail makes no charge for enquiries and registers itself just once; why not force all organizations to follow this example?

Making the Act more user-friendly

Why not reverse the burden of investigation from the individual onto the organization? Why not create a Data Subject's Charter to define what data an organization is obliged to give individuals? After all, this is what your bank does when you ask them for a statement of your account — you get a complete record of your transactions with them over the last period. You should be able to obtain a similar service from, say, a direct mail organization. Isn't this how the Act really should work?

Basically, all this requires is two things:

1. Customer-focused systems, so that it is possible to go straight to the (computerized) file relating to an individual.
2. Clear definitions of what sort of information the individual is entitled to know.

Like phoning your bank to check your account, making an enquiry via the Data Protection Act should be quick and simple.

But what is a customer-focused system? The best way to describe it is to describe first its opposite, a data-centred system. Data-centred systems are the sort of systems which exist in most organizations today. They are designed to give maximum efficiency to an organization's data processing requirements — data is organized by function (inventory, sales, accounts and so on), not by customer, and the systems automate the data-flows between these functions. To make a customer enquiry in such an environment is obviously possible (it is done every day), but the enquiry will be specific to a system and the answer provided may not be in a form which suits the customer (for example, a credit rating which is an incomprehensible code).

Customer-focused systems, on the other hand, organize data around the customer. Enquiring on a customer record in such a system will give access to all aspects of the customer's dealings with the organization — their address, their order details, delivery dates, payment records, any correspondence, etc. You can see how the quality of customer service in general, and data protection in particular, would improve in this environment.

There is a strong movement towards implementing the customer-focused model in organizations. By exploiting this trend, the Data Protection Act could gain greatly in terms of customer acceptability.

Reducing national security exemptions and strengthening the Act

The exemptions to the Act may decrease due to three tendencies:

1. The denationalization of many Government agencies: as this happens, Government, cynically, is less concerned about protecting these functions.
2. A small movement towards more open Government.
3. The impact of the European Union.

The first two tendencies are rather weak. For example, a Government agency may be denationalized only to be swallowed up by an anti-democratic multinational company. Individuals need to use the Act as a means of keeping pressure on Government and organizations to be more open, rather than simply waiting for things to improve.

The impact of the European Union on data protection in the UK could be substantial. There is a European Union directive on data protection, which at the time of writing has yet to be adopted in the UK, which recognizes, as a fundamental right, the privacy of individuals in relation to data processing. It lays down strict laws governing the use of such data. It also proposes to widen the scope of legislation to include data held on paper files. Even more radically, it proposes that individuals have to provide their consent to permit use of personal data. Individuals must also be told at the time of collection what the data is to be used for and be given the name and address of the database controller!

Whether all of these proposals are ultimately practical, the thinking behind them is to be welcomed. They show how the Act is likely to develop in future, towards greater power for the individual data subject. The idea that the Data Protection Act is an irrelevance will become less and less true.

3.6 Conclusions

We have suggested that the Data Protection Act needs radical changes if it is to gain the full support both of the public and of organizations.

We concluded that the Act would work better if there was less time spent on maintaining the registration process and more on monitoring compliance with the Principles.

We pointed out that the Data Protection Act is not a Freedom of Information Act, Privacy Act or the like. These pieces of legislation are needed separately.

We suggested that organizations should, in their own interest, be more positive towards the Act; they should see it as part and parcel of their adoption of the customer-focused model.

We said that software engineers need to take on board the Data Protection Principles to meet the law as it now stands. We reviewed each Principle in turn and noted that they have real implications for systems design.

Finally, we said that the Act is unlikely to disappear — whatever its faults, it is too useful to do that. In fact its role will grow over time, particularly in response to additional European Union legislation.

About the author

Dave Pitt is a Senior Business Consultant with AT&T Global Information Solutions, the new $70 billion company formed from the merger of NCR Computers and AT&T. He has part-time responsibility for the UK company's compliance with the Data Protection Act.

Note that AT&T have recently adopted a "casual dress policy" to reflect their desire for a modern, unstuffy image; so the author is open to offers for his wardrobe of Armani suits and would like to purchase the following items: trainers (laces not required), Levi cut-offs, T-shirt (ecologically-correct slogan preferred) and baseball cap (must look good when worn back-to-front).

Further reading

Bainbridge D. (1990), *Computers and the Law*, Pitman.

Booth N. (1992), *PCLAN*, June 1992.

Campbell D. (1988), *On and Off the Record*, Personal Computer World, October 1988.

The Data Protection Act 1984, HMSO.

Kanter R. (1992), *When Giants Dance*, Routledge.

Smith M. (1991), *Software Prototyping*, McGraw-Hill.

Tazelaar J. (1990), *Object Lessons*, Byte, October 1990.

FOUR

AVOIDING A SOFTWARE LAWSUIT
BY LIZ DUFF

4.1 Introduction

This chapter introduces those areas of law that are specifically relevant to the software engineer. There are, of course, many other areas of law of which they ought to be aware (such as Health and Safety legislation and Employment law). However, these areas should be known to everyone — not just the software engineer and consequently are not dealt with here.

Before dealing with any specific issues, it is important to stress the fact that this chapter can only highlight those legal aspects that are important to software engineers: it cannot replace good legal advice. As a professional one needs to appreciate that the law relating to computer technology is changing rapidly when compared with most other areas of law. This "newness" has two important consequences:

1. Although, often an unfair perspective, the law is not always considered adequate to deal with the problems thrown up by the new technology.
2. Members of the legal profession have a variable level of experience with respect to how the law relates to information technology. This means that the software engineer must be careful to select a solicitor with an appropriate level of expertise.

With these provisos is mind, this chapter will discuss:

1. The consequences of negligent software design.
2. Contractual considerations and obligations for the software developer.
3. Liability under the Computer Misuse Act 1990.
4. Intellectual property rights in software.

4.2 Negligence

It is probable that some software engineers will find themselves threatened with an action under the *tort of negligence*. An action in negligence is a civil matter, and arises when someone is damaged or injured due to a breach in the standard of behaviour required by law, by another person who is considered to be responsible for that damage or injury. Two points are worth noting:

1. The tort of negligence is an offence in *civil law*. This means that the action normally will be taken by an *individual* for harm they consider has been caused to them. By contrast, an offence under *criminal law* will be brought on behalf of the State.
2. The tort of negligence is an area of *common law*. That is, a court will have decided the legality of a particular action, which will then form the basis to determine the legality of other similar cases. This has an important consequence for software engineers: information technology is a new technology and so there often will be little precedence to establish the legality of an action under this tort. Hence, legal actions may prove costly and time-consuming.

The following case study shows how an act of negligence might arise, and discusses what measures may be taken to avoid it.

4.2.1 Case study — Drill and Fill

As the owner of Slick Software, you were contracted to provide software for a dental practice 'Drill and Fill'. The program was required to calculate a patient's treatment costs; including any subsidy from the National Health Service (NHS), and the total amount owed by the patient at the end of the course of treatment. In addition, the program had to send out letters informing patients of their next check-up appointment.

The program was completed eighteen months ago and you provide updates of the system to the practice, which allow them to amend the NHS subsidy.

Unfortunately, a problem has arisen. It appears that the Appointments System for notifying patients of their check-ups has a bug, and approximately 5% of patients have not been receiving their notifications. One patient, Ms Suet, claims that due to missing her check-up, an abscess is much worse than it might have been, with the result that she needs to have the tooth removed and replaced with a bridge. Ms Drill of the dental practice agrees that the patient's condition could indeed have deteriorated due to the delay.

The dental practice have successfully convinced the patient that the whole incident is not their fault, but yours, as the software provider. The claim is that due to your negligence in designing the software, the patient has suffered damage and loss of her tooth that could otherwise have been avoided, had she been called for her appointment on time.

4.2.2 Is there a claim in negligence?

In order to sue for negligence the patient, Ms Suet, needs to establish three essential elements:

1. Duty of Care
2. Breach of duty
3. Harm was caused due to the breach of duty.

First, Ms Suet must show that she was owed a legal duty by the software engineer; this is known as a *Duty of Care*. In general, anyone involved in designing or manufacturing goods is obliged to take reasonable care in their design or manufacture. This duty extends beyond the immediate user (in the above case, Drill and Fill) to include anyone who might foreseeably be injured by its use (in the above case, it could be argued this encompasses all the patients of the dental practice).

Second, Ms Suet would have to prove that the software engineer had been in breach of a Duty of Care. This legal duty is not absolute: a court will take into account the circumstances of the case, and will consider the degree of care that should be taken in relation to the risk of harm. For liability to arise there must be some element of negligence. This means that the software engineer has not acted as a reasonably competent engineer would. Clearly, this part of the claim is the hardest to prove as the potential victim has the difficult evidential burden of establishing that the engineer had been negligent.

Third, Ms Suet would have to prove that it was due to the negligence of the software engineer that she was harmed, and, in addition, that it was the type of harm that was foreseeable. In the above case, this means that Ms Suet would need medical evidence to support her claim that she had to have her tooth removed because the lateness of her treatment aggravated her condition. Furthermore, she would have to establish that it was reasonable to assume that the bug in the Appointments System would lead to a late check-up which would then lead to the aggravated abscess. In Slick Software's defence, it could be argued that she should have felt the abscess and sought treatment immediately rather than wait for a check-up.

Assuming that the claim in negligence has been successful then a court will award damages which represent the losses which are reasonably foreseeable consequences of the breach.

4.2.3 Financial or physical loss?

Where someone suffers physical injury, the law allows a claim for damages. However, where the loss suffered is purely financial, it is more difficult for the victim to succeed. Consider the situation where Ms Suet, instead of suffering tooth removal, had only incurred additional expenses because of price increases which could have been avoided had she been called for treatment earlier. Here, there is no physical damage because of the late check-up appointment, there is only the financial loss, representing the difference in price for the same treatment.

To succeed in a claim of negligence in such a case, the law requires that there be a special relationship between the parties: such as that between an accountant and a client or a solicitor and a house buyer.

4.2.4 Defences to a claim of negligence

Competent as any software engineer

Since the duty under negligence is not absolute, that is, the software engineer is required to take only reasonable care, it is possible to raise the defence that such care has been taken by establishing that the program was of the same standard as that provided by any competent software engineer.

Furthermore, there may be practical considerations; such as whether the program has been operated correctly by the staff at the dental practice.

Contracting out of liability

It might be possible to avoid some liability by drafting an appropriate contract between the engineer and the client. In this situation, it is essential for the software engineer to specify what can be expected of the program and what defects might arise. By bringing to the client's attention any possible defects, these defects become part of the agreed program specification and cannot be the basis of a negligence action.

However, under the Unfair Contract Terms Act 1977, it it is not permissible to exclude or restrict liability if, as a result of negligence, death or personal injury occurs. In this situation, liability is *imposed* and there is *no defence*. The producer will be liable even if they can prove that they took all reasonable care to check the product.

Additional liability under the Consumer Protection Act

The Consumer Protection Act 1987 requires that a producer shall be liable for damage caused by a defect in their product. An important aspect is that it can only be used where the property damaged as a result of defects was ordinarily intended for private use and exceeds £275 in value. For example, a claim could not be brought under this statute against a software engineer who had designed a program for an industrial saw, if the program is then found to be flawed, causing damage to the saw and making it operate incorrectly. It is immaterial that the damage caused amounts to over £275. However, if the saw operator is injured as a result of the defective program, there is no such avoidance and the software engineer would be liable. The statute creates absolute liability for death or personal injury due to a defective product.

Defences to the Consumer Protection Act

There are a number of defences laid down in the Consumer Protection Act 1987, but the most important for the software engineer would be that called the "state of the art defence". This defence can be used where the producer can show that there was no scientific or technical knowledge, at the time the product was developed, to suggest that this defect would occur. However, it would be unwise to rely on this approach because the courts do not easily accept such a defence.

4.3 Contractual considerations

4.3.1 Software licences

If a software engineer is developing a program for someone with a specific purpose in mind, it is essential that there is a document which states the obligations of the parties to the agreement. An overriding consideration for software engineers is that the document is drafted fairly, so that the terms are not over-onerous for them, and that they have adequate protection under the agreement.

The agreement which is drawn up is usually a specific form of contract known as a *software licence*. The reason why licences are used rather than *contracts of sale* is that software is subject to *intellectual property rights*, and by using a licence a degree of control can be exercised over the program (see Section 4.6.4).

Programs that are developed under such an agreement are referred to as 'bespoke software': that is, programs which are tailor-made to users' requirements rather than general-purpose software that is bought off the shelf.

4.3.2 Who owns the program?

A software licence is of particular importance where software has been commissioned. It is common practice to find that in such situations the contract states that the intellectual property rights are owned by the client who commissioned the program and not the engineer. This is obviously a very important matter that should be addressed when drafting the bespoke licence agreement.

In fact, it is now established in English law that the copyright does not belong to the commissioner of the software but to the "author". If the software engineer intends to pass all legal interests in the program to the commissioning party, then this must be clearly stated in the form of an *exclusive licence*. Such an agreement should be reflected in the price paid for the software by the commissioner of the work. If the commissioner does not have such a licence, the software engineer could exploit it to make greater profits by licensing the program to a competitor of the commissioner. Although a lot depends upon the relative bargaining strength of the parties, it is likely that the commissioner would seek to prevent the software engineer from exploiting the program in this way.

4.3.3 The user's requirement

When drafting a software licence it is essential that both the software engineer and the user have a clear understanding of what is required and incorporate this into the document. This entails an unambiguous explanation of the user's requirement. Which is easier said than done! Indeed, probably the hardest task facing the software profession is not writing the code but deciding what code to write.

Where the software is complex and the user may need to amend the specification, this should be dealt with in the licence, allowing extra time and payment to the software engineer.

4.3.4 Completion dates and maintenance

The licence should also cater for a completion date for the program, with perhaps some consideration if additional time is needed for amendments should the client wish to re-establish their requirements.

Generally, the licence will also cover maintenance of the software. Even though "bugs" are virtually inevitable they are strictly a minor breach of contract, therefore, there should be some provision regarding how long after installation that the software engineer will be responsible for rectifying these problems without extra payment or an additional agreement.

4.3.5 Acceptance testing

The client will probably want to include an acceptance testing clause. This is very important as it gives the user the opportunity to establish whether the software engineer has indeed provided the software as stated in the contract and, perhaps more importantly, if they are entitled to payment.

4.3.6 Client security and escrow

As a final safety net the client may want an independent third party to have a source code copy of the program to cover situations such as the software engineer going out of business. This will enable the client or another third party to continue to maintain the software. The National Computing Centre is one organization which provides such an *escrow* service.

4.3.7 Protection for the developer

The software engineer should take some basic precautions to ensure that their liability is not excessive when negotiating the terms of the licence. The following is not intended to be an exhaustive list of precautions but is an indication of the major issues that should be considered:

1. Software developers might want to ensure that their users get appropriate training; inadequately trained personnel are a major source of complaints.
2. As stated earlier in this chapter, limitation of liability in negligence and contract should be considered. Liability under these two areas can sometimes be excluded, but it is more likely to be successful if the contract term seeks to limit liability.

   As may be expected, use of such terms is tightly controlled by law. If software engineers insert such clauses in a contract, they should note that such a term will be construed against them, meaning, any clause must be clearly expressed. In a contract between businesses, the software engineer could be protected for liability arising from a breach of contract only if the term were reasonable.†

3. If the software is to be supplied to an individual consumer the law is even more protective of their interests, stating that liability for death and personal injury arising from negligence cannot be excluded in the contract. In addition, liability under statutes which give individual consumers contractual rights cannot be excluded, for example that goods must be fit for their purpose, and that any work must be carried out with reasonable care and skill.

4.3.8 Insurance

It is very important that the software engineer has adequate insurance cover. Insurance contracts are not necessarily clearly worded, therefore it is advisable to ascertain what is covered by the insurers. Some insurers might be reluctant to cover the software engineer who is developing a program with a high degree of risk, for instance a legal expert system. It is always advisable to ensure that liability under the Consumer Protection Act 1987 is included. When the statute first came into operation some insurers had difficulty categorizing the risks involved.

4.3.9 Professional advice

It must be emphasized that the software engineer should seek the professional assistance of an independent solicitor with experience of software contracts to advise them on the scope of the licence and any contractual issues.

4.4 Criminal offences

The first sections of this chapter have dealt with *civil* liability, where software engineers could find themselves being sued for damages owing to defects in the quality of their work. However, they could also find themselves with *criminal* liability, and subject to police investigation, with the possibility of punishment by a custodial sentence.

This section provides a basic overview of the three offences created by the Computer Misuse Act 1990; it will not address issues such as fraud and false accounting perpetrated by computer. The author assumes that

---

† Unfair Contract Terms Act 1977, Section 3. What is reasonable is determined by statute taking into account the bargaining position of the parties, any reliance placed on the other's expertise, whether the goods were specifically made for the buyer etc.

the reader is ethical and only requires guidance as to the nature of offences that accidentally may be committed.

The Computer Misuse Act was introduced to address the problems of gaining unauthorized access to computer systems from a remote computer, often referred to as "hacking". The Act created three new offences:

1. **Basic hacking** to obtain access to programs or data without intention to carry out a further act.
2. **Obtaining unauthorized access** with the intent to commit a further offence, such as fraud or blackmail.
3. **Unauthorized modification** of the contents of any computer.

These offences carry different levels of punishment which relate to the respective seriousness of the offence. The basic hacking offence carries a maximum fine of £5000 or a prison sentence not exceeding six months. The offences carry a maximum penalty of a five-year custodial sentence.

Given that law-abiding software engineers are unlikely to want to 'hack', they might find it difficult to understand the relevance of this Act to them. The rest of this section outlines how they might find themselves unintentionally involved.

4.4.1 Case study — Hackit and Die

Slick Software have been approached by the editor of *Hackit* magazine, a publication for Internet users. *Hackit* want Slick to write a program which will assist its readers in gaining access to databases which are protected by passwords. The program is required to break through this password protection. The program will be sold through the magazine. Slick Software have two employees working on the project for three weeks when they give a copy of the program to *Hackit* for their perusal. *Hackit* appear pleased with the software which they call *Breaker* and agree to pay £2500 for the program. They give Slick £250 and promise them the balance one month later. Three months later Slick have still not been paid. One of the employees who worked on the Breaker program visits the premises of *Hackit*, and tells the editor of the magazine that there is a bug in the program and they would like to modify it. Whilst on the premises the Slick employee gains access to the network and sets a password, preventing use of the entire network of *Hackit*. Slick contact *Hackit* and tell them that if they pay the outstanding £2250 they will remove the password.

4.4.2 Issues arising

This situation might give rise to criminal liability. First, with regard to the Breaker program, the magazine could find itself liable for incitement to commit the Section 1 criminal offence of obtaining unauthorized access to a computer or data, in other words "hacking". The magazine would be providing the means by which a person could defeat a security system. However, the software engineers of Slick might also find themselves criminally liable for having devised the means by which the hacker can obtain access. This is a difficult area of criminal law, and the best advice for the software engineer would be not to become involved in such an enterprise.

As regards the placing of a password on the network of *Hackit* by the employee of Slick, this might well amount to a Section 3 offence under the Computer Misuse Act 1990. This is where there is unauthorized modification of data or a program. This particular type of activity — the setting of software locks — has been considered by the courts, and disillusioned engineers have been found guilty under Section 3.

In summary, it is highly unlikely that an ethical software engineer will find themselves in the position of having committed an offence under the Computer Misuse Act. It should be noted how widely drafted is Section 1, it is an offence to hack into a system even if you have no intention of doing anything else. It is sufficient that you have gained unauthorized access and you are liable to be found guilty of the Section 1 offence.

If you provide someone with the means to commit any of the offences under the Computer Misuse Act 1990 there is the possibility that you could be found to have committed an incitement to commit a crime or to be an accomplice to the crime.

4.5 Intellectual property rights

The rest of this chapter covers the ways in which the law provides protection for software. The law recognizes that a computer program is worthy of protection because it is the result of creative energy and considerable work; and is therefore protected as an intellectual property right. The following issues will be considered:

1. How software obtains copyright protection
2. The appropriateness of patent protection for software
3. Protection of the idea behind software — breach of confidence

4.6 Copyright

The primary area of protection for software is that of copyright. Copyright is an attractive means of protection as there are no formalities to fulfil and no registration or form filling is required. Copyright protection is provided from the moment the author of the work records it in some form. The current legislation is the Copyright, Designs and Patents Act 1988, hereinafter referred to as the CDPA 1988. Copyright is a property right which exists in a number of "works", these works include original literary works, films and sound recordings. A computer program is classified in this Act as a "literary work". The requirements that the "work" needs to acquire copyright are:

1. Originality
2. Tangibility
3. Qualification
4. Ownership

The following case study illustrates these requirements and explains the measures that can be taken if copyright is infringed.

4.6.1 Case study — Mick is sick

Mick is a self-employed software engineer. He is approached by Merlin Accounting Systems to write a package appropriate for one of their clients, an optician called Boggle Eyes. The package is required to work out clients' appointments, bills etc. Mick personalized the package so that every document had the Boggle Eyes logo and telephone number on it. He completed the work and was paid £3000. Mick later became aware that Merlin had rewritten the program using a different language — making some minor amendments to its behaviour — and were now advertising the package for £500 to opticians' practices.

4.6.2 Is there copyright in the program?

Originality

Mick must establish that the work is "original". The meaning of "original" in terms of copyright does not mean that it has to be new, but simply requires that the work is the product of the author's efforts, and that is that it is not copied. It would appear that Mick has met with this requirement.

Tangibility

Copyright can only protect the expression of an idea, and not the idea itself. Therefore, it is an essential condition that the work be recorded in some way. Since this is a very broad requirement, it clearly encompasses a computer program because as soon as it is saved on to either a hard or floppy disk, it has been recorded "in writing or otherwise" (Section 3(2) CDPA). Again, Mick can meet this requirement because Merlin has received from him a copy of the program on disk.

Qualification

There is a qualification requirement that must be satisfied before copyright can subsist in the work. The qualification can be met in one of two ways, by reference either to the author of the work or to the country where it was first published. Usually this is not a problem, because this requirement is easily satisfied where the work is created by a UK citizen or a person domiciled or resident in the UK. In addition, there are two international copyright conventions, the Berne and Unversal Copyright conventions, which provide reciprocal protection to works that would otherwise not qualify. The UK is a signatory to both these conventions. It is, therefore, unlikely that a person writing software in the UK would not be protected. It can be assumed for the purposes of this case study that Mick is a citizen of the UK, domiciled in the UK.

Ownership

The effect of copyright is to provide protection for the author, who is usually the person who has created the work (although it might be their employer). Copyright subsists for a period of fifty years after the author's death. The problem for Mick is to establish that he did not intend to transfer the ownership in the copyright to Merlin. This is where the contract between Merlin and Mick becomes vital. If Mick intended to give ownership of the copyright in the program it should have been stated clearly in the contract. (See Section 4.3.2 above.)

Is there infringement?

If it is accepted that Mick is the owner of the copyright, he will then need to establish that Merlin have infringed his rights. As the copyright owner Mick has exclusive rights to do the following:

1. Copy the work
2. Issue copies of the work to the public
3. Perform, show or play the work in public
4. To broadcast the work or include it in a cable television programme

5. To make an adaptation of the work or do any of the above in relation to an adaptation.

If it is established that Merlin did any of the above actions they have infringed Mick's copyright.

If Merlin have copied the program from one disk to another this amounts to copying, and establishes infringement. However, in Mick's case the situation is more complex. It would appear that Merlin has not just copied the program but has rewritten the program using the structure and routines that he had developed for Boggle Eyes. This process is called *non-literal copying*. To establish that this process has taken place would be difficult for Mick if he decided that he wanted to pursue an infringement action through the courts. The procedure is long and expensive. The court would compare the non-literal elements of the program (a literal comparison would not be useful as the programs are written in different languages). The non-literal elements include the structure and sequence, the input and output routines, menus and format. This type of analysis is known as the "look and feel" of the program. If the judges were satisfied that some of these non-literal elements had been copied Mick would be able to establish infringement. However, the court will consider that there can be no copyright of material where there is only one way to express an idea, or that there is only one way to carry out a particular function.

In addition, Mick may be able to claim that Merlin have made an adaptation of his program. The CDPA 1988 specifically deals with the situation where a computer program "is converted into or out of a computer language or code into a different language or code" (Section 21(4) CDPA 1988).

It should be noted that there are situations where it is lawful to make copies and adaptations of a program. These situations were introduced by the EC Directive on the Legal Protection of Computer Programs. As a result of this directive three new sections were introduced into the CDPA 1988. These exceptions to a claim of infringement only apply to lawful users of the program. If Merlin wanted to rely upon the exceptions provided by these sections they would first need to establish that they were lawful users of the program.

4.6.3 Remedies for infringement

If Mick is the owner of the copyright to the program he has the right to bring an action for infringement. This action is a civil matter and is referred to as a tort for breach of a statutory duty. It should be noted that if Merlin had been granted an exclusive licence they would have the right to bring an action. The remedies available for infringement are:

1. Damages
2. Injunctions
3. Account of profits

Mick would claim damages to put himself in the position he would have been in had the tort not been committed (see Section 4.2.3). Injunctions are used to prohibit the repetition of a tort. An "account of profits" is not commonly sought. This remedy is claimed when the defendant has made a great deal of money from the infringement, and is claimed instead of damages. There are criminal offences associated with infringement of copyright. These are of a commercial nature and involve dealing with infringing copies of the work.

4.6.4 Avoiding the pitfalls — what Mick should have done

To avoid a dispute Mick should have drawn up a contract with the help of a solicitor who has experience of this type of agreement. In the above case study, Mick could have decided to transfer the ownership rights in the program to Merlin: this is by means of an *assignment of copyright*. Such an agreement is required by law to be in writing. An assignment can be of limited duration, perhaps twenty-five years; or refer to one aspect of the work. Thus books may have an assignment of rights in the hardback edition but not in the paperback.

An alternative arrangement that Mick could have entered into is to have a *licence agreement* with Merlin. A licence does not transfer ownership in any of the copyright, it permits acts that would otherwise amount to infringement. An exclusive licence allows the licensee to do an act that even the owner of the copyright cannot do. It is possible to grant a non-exclusive licence, a licence granting the same rights can be granted to a number of people. An example of this type of licence is that which is issued when one purchases a copy of Microsoft Windows.

Clearly, if Mick and Merlin had entered into one of the above agreements, any dispute could have been avoided.

4.6.5 Interoperability and copyright

Software engineers when providing a program for a client need a great deal of information from the client (see Section 4.3.3) and from other sources. They will also need to know the operating system that the client is using and any other programs with which the new program needs to be compatible, this is known as *interoperability of programs*. Hence, in the above case study, Mick may need to know the accounts and word-processing package used by Boggle Eyes if he is to write an effective program for them. The newly inserted Section 50B in the CDPA allows

Mick to decompile the accounts and word-processing programs to obtain, for instance, interface details of those programs. The information obtained can only be used to create an independent program to be used in conjunction with another program. As a result of the new Section 50B, decompilation for this purpose would not amount to infringement of copyright.

4.6.6 Computer-generated works

The software engineer should be aware of the law regarding computer-generated works. These are defined in the CDPA 1988 as work that is "generated by computer in circumstances such that there is no human author" (Section 178 CDPA 1988). One problem is how to distinguish between work that has a human author, for instance the program, and work that is created by that program. A good example of a computer-generated work is that of an expert system — who has authorship and ownership of a report produced using one of these programs? It is essential to establish who is the author because this establishes ownership of the copyright in the computer-generated works. In addition, where the work is created by a computer, copyright runs for fifty years from the end of the year in which the work was created, not from when the author dies. Unfortunately, since the CDPA 1988 came into force there have been no decisions which have clarified this point.

4.7 Patent protection

One method of protection for a computer program is by way of patent law. The granting of a patent is attractive as it gives monopoly rights to the patent holder over the subject matter of the patent. Patents are especially appropriate to inventions. If a program is to be granted patent protection it must meet the requirements laid down in the Patents Act 1977, which are as follows:

1. The invention must be new.
2. There must be an inventive step.
3. It is capable of industrial application.
4. It is not excluded by the Act.

A computer program is excluded from patent protection by Section 1(2) of the Patents Act. There have been a number of failed attempts to establish the patentability of software. It now seems clear that the appropriate means of protecting a program is by means of copyright.

4.8 Breach of confidence

Breach of confidence is another action under tort, and is a civil matter. This is an attractive option as just like copyright there are no formalities to be met, and in theory the information can be kept secret or confidential, for an indefinite period.

4.8.1 Case study — A Chinese Puzzle

Kim has written a program that can translate Mandarin Chinese into English. The Mandarin Chinese can be scanned into the computer using a hand-held scanner, then the program translates this information into English. Kim is a university teacher and does not know how to go about selling and marketing her program, or even if it would have any commercial value. Kim approaches Big Bucks Ltd, a software distribution company, with a view to them marketing her program in the future.

Kim meets with one of Big Bucks' representatives and explains how her program works, its hardware requirements and other relevant details. Big Bucks contact Kim after the meeting and explain that although her program was interesting, the market for such a product is probably in China and they do not have any business contacts there.

Six months later, Kim finds out from a friend that Big Bucks have employed a software engineer to write a program that will behave in the same manner as her program.

Since Big Bucks Ltd have not yet completed the writing of the software, the best course of action for Kim is to sue them for breach of confidence and to seek an injunction preventing them from disclosing her ideas for the translation program. To successfully claim that there had been a breach of confidence Kim would have to establish the following:

1. The imparted information must have the necessary quality of confidence about it; that is, the information must not be public property or be knowledge in the public domain.
2. The information must have been imparted in circumstances indicating an obligation of confidence.
3. There must be an unauthorized use of that information to the detriment of the party communicating it.

Considering each of the above points in turn:

1. Kim has told Big Bucks Ltd about her program, which is clearly information not known to the public. Therefore, it can be established that the information has the quality of confidence.

2. The second requirement has also been satisfied. Confidence is assumed in relationships such as doctor and patient but it can be extended to business negotiations.
3. Finally, it is obvious that Big Bucks Ltd have used the information to the detriment of Kim. If they had their own program based on Kim's idea and then marketed it, this would negatively affect Kim's prospect of commercially exploiting her program.

If a court were satisfied that Kim had met the three conditions it could grant her an injunction against Big Bucks Ltd preventing them from using the information she gave them. If, however, Big Bucks had already began to sell their version of the translation program, Kim may be able to claim damages. Because the information has been used in a commercial enterprise, Kim may be entitled to make a claim for an account of profits instead of damages.

4.9 Summary

This chapter introduced the basic legal issues that are of importance to a software engineer. It is intended to act as warning to the complex nature of the law that relates to the development of software, and to emphasize the potential liability and the vulnerability of the software engineer. The second part of this chapter outlines the mechanisms provided for software engineers to protect their programs, so that they might be able to exploit them commercially — before someone else does.

About the author

Liz Duff is a senior lecturer in Law at the University of Westminster, specializing in contract, tort and computers and the law.

She once claimed a tax allowance on special clothes for lecturing (bullet-proof vest and a hard-hat). This had the same lack of success as the claim made by a solicitor for having to wear sombre clothes during court-room activities.

Further reading

Bainbridge D. (1994), *Intellectual Property Law (2nd edition)*, Pitman.

Bainbridge D. (1993), *Introduction to Computer Law (2nd edition)*, Pitman.

Bainbridge D. (1992), *Software Copyright Law*, Pitman.

Dworkin D. and Taylor R. (1988), *Copyright Designs and Patent Act*, Blackstone Press.

Lloyd I. (1993), *Information Technology Law*, Butterworths.

Oughton D. (1991), *Consumer Law, Text, Cases and Materials*, Blackstone Press.

Reed C. (1993), *Computer Law (2nd edition)*, Blackstone Press.

Robertson R. (1990), *Legal Protection of Computer Software*, Longman.

Tapper C. (1989), *Computer Law (4th edition)*, Longman.

FIVE

PITY THE POOR USER
BY HILARY HUSBAND

5.1 Introducing a new computer system

Suppose you have designed a system which meets the required specification and which has been tried successfully in several workplaces.
You may believe that your system is going to help people, make their
work easier or enable them to use information more efficiently. When
the system is introduced to new users you find they start to complain.
The users may be resistant, and the more the virtues of the system are
explained, the more resistant and antagonistic they become. Problems
will be encountered whenever a new system is introduced, even one
which has been well tried and tested. This chapter is concerned with the
tensions that may arise when a system is introduced.

There are a range of variables which mediate the success, or otherwise, with which a new system may be introduced into the workplace.
Prospective users may be misinformed, prejudiced or threatened by the
introduction of the system. The people who have to use the system are
often not the people who have asked for it. The request for the system
may have come from "management" and may be something users feel
is being imposed upon them. You need to understand not only what is
wanted by management but also the fears and concerns (both realistic
and unrealistic) of the prospective users.

5.1.1 Organizational demands

To illustrate some of these fears and concerns a hypothetical example of what can happen when a system is introduced will be described. Before considering the difficulties encountered by users themselves we need to consider the organization in which they work.

Organizations can (and do) have complicated management structures and demands for systems can be generated from various points in these structures. The needs of one part of the organization may be entirely different from those of another part.

There is the formal, acknowledged, management structure but there is also the informal structure to be considered. The most powerful and influential person may not be "The Manager" who wields formal power but the secretary who controls access to him or her. A basic knowledge of the management structure and culture of the organization with which you are working is essential.

Prospective users may have other agendas or problems which are preoccupying them at the time when the system is being introduced. There may be other important and major changes happening concomitantly with their working practices. To varying degrees, different individuals may view a new computer system as irrelevant to their current needs or a further major complication they could do without. The computer system may be seen as a tool introduced by the managers to bring about a more global, unpopular change in working practices. In extreme cases, the computer system can itself come to symbolize all the problems currently being experienced by workers in the organization. Before the system is introduced find out what other changes the prospective users may be struggling with. Is now a good time? And if not, why not?

5.2 The Community Health Team

To illustrate these problems let us take an example. Our hypothetical example concerns a Community Health Team in a rural area. Before meeting the individuals in the Team we need to examine the history and functions of the Team.

The Community Health Team has been running for about two years when the Health Authority decides to introduce a district-wide Patient Information and Administration System (PIAS). This will be used by all the Community Health Teams in the Health Authority. The last two years have been a period of rapid change and difficult re-adjustment for all the individuals in the Team. The Team has been formed from a group of existing health care professionals who had previously had little contact with each other. They have come to be based in a rural Health

Centre, sharing a large open-plan office, secretaries and communal interview/treatment rooms. The Team consists of Community Nurses, Physiotherapists, Midwives, Community Psychiatric Nurses, Occupational Therapists and Health Visitors. In the last two years they have had to start working collaboratively, sharing casework, liaising, consulting and networking. There have been professional jealousies, territorial disputes and personality clashes. Disputes arose over which members of the Team can have "key worker" responsibility for patients. It was received wisdom that the CPN (Community Psychiatric Nurse) and the OT (Occupational Therapist) did not get on. At one time the Midwives would not allow the Health Visitors to use their kettle. To further complicate matters there are sessional visits from a Clinical Psychologist, a Social Worker, a Speech Therapist and a Dietician.

Many of the competencies and skills of the Team members are shared and there are areas of overlap as well as specialist skills and knowledge. The Team is often called a Multi-Disciplinary Team and the Team Leader or Manager may be drawn from any one of the professional groups represented within the Team.

The Manager of the Team is a Senior Nurse. This did not go down well with non-nurse members of the Team. Those Team members who are not nurses receive professional line-management from senior members of their own professional discipline — who are based geographically distant from the Health Centre. The sessional visitors have their own obscure management arrangements. Whilst the Team has frequent internal disagreements it has evolved sufficiently to provide a united front to change imposed from outside or above.

The Community Team is a small part of a much larger, highly complex organization. It is one of a series of Community Health Teams located throughout the district. These other teams also have their problems. Community Health Teams are just one way in which services are delivered to patients in the Health Authority. There are also, for example, Acute General Hospitals, Psychiatric Hospitals and Services for the Mentally Handicapped.

Let us meet some of the members of the Team. George Conning is a Senior Nurse and the Manager of the Team. He is a quiet man in his early forties who does not enjoy conflict. He often feels his loyalties are split between the Team he manages and the Clinical Director of Community Services to whom he is answerable. Whilst he believes that most members of the Team respect and like him, he has particular difficulties with Bill Thurlow, the CPN. Bill is a rather abrasive, forceful personality who resents the fact that he had not been appointed as Team Manager himself. Bill is a few years older that George, and his prospects of further promotion are limited. George sometimes thinks that Bill considers him to be rather weak in his dealings with the Clinical Director. It isn't that

George dislikes Bill, far from it, but he does wish Bill could be a little less offensive in the way he expressed his views at times. Perhaps as the only two men in a Team comprised mainly of females they were bound to clash from time to time.

5.2.1 The meeting

When George arrived at the Health Centre on Monday morning he slipped into his office unobserved. The previous week he had been on an "away-a-day" with other Team Managers to learn about the new computer system. It had been a good day. Some managers from another Health Authority already using the system had given a presentation. George had been impressed by the system. The NHS reforms, as the Clinical Director had explained, made a first-rate computer system imperative. Whilst George did not agree with all the NHS changes he thought the computer system had a lot of benefits to bring to his Team. It was likely to make his job of monitoring work-loads and patient care procedures considerably easier. There had been plans to get the Information Technology Manager to introduce the system to the Team members. George had thought it over and decided to undertake the first briefing himself. The Team might feel a bit intimidated by an IT Manager — frightened of asking stupid questions or showing their ignorance of computer technology. No-one could be frightened of showing their ignorance to him, he reasoned, he was almost as uninformed as they were. George knew that the Team knew the system was coming. He was close enough to them to be aware of the gossip and rumours which circulated in the staff room. It just wasn't possible to keep a big issue like this under wraps for very long. Certainly not when Bill Thurlow had a habit of reading any correspondence left on his desk! George called a meeting for that afternoon. He could spend the rest of the morning reading over what he already knew about the system. One thing was sure, the Team wouldn't be greeting the news that the system was on its way with universal glee and jubilation.

When George arrived at the meeting room it was deserted. The two Midwives had left a note on the table apologizing for not being able to attend. They were both involved in home deliveries. It was always a problem getting the whole Team together. He started to assemble the coffee machine — an archaic contraption resembling an incontinent Dalek which was the object of much derision from the staff. He took a private bet with himself as to who would be the first to arrive.

In the event it was Ann, the Physiotherapist. He liked Ann, she was straightforward and easy to get on with.

"Hello George", she said, "don't tell me everyone else is late — I broke my neck trying to get here by one-thirty."

George grinned. One of the games the Team liked to play was trying to be the last to arrive at any meeting. The person who achieved this coveted aim could then imply that they were the busiest member of the Team, dealing with the most urgent clinical problems.

Bill was the next to arrive, bearing a huge bundle of patients' notes.

"You certainly pick the most inconvenient times George — I'm up to my eyeballs in work at the moment", he announced, sizing up the seating arrangements and choosing a place which gave him a commanding view of the car park. "Betty's on her way", he added.

Betty Hislop, the District Nurse, entered the room. She did not look happy.

"If this is about computers George", she began, "just you remember that some of us are a bit long in the tooth to start learning about them. After all — I retire in two years." Betty folded her arms as if to indicate that was all she had to say on the subject.

"We have got a lot of other things to worry about at the moment", said Ann, "not just physiotherapists, but all of us. Like getting to grips with becoming an NHS Trust and the Community Care Act."

George knew that this was true.

Louise Rackman, the OT (Occupational Therapist), Sharon Frost, a Nursing Assistant and Janice Dent, the Team Secretary entered.

"Sorry George, but the Health Visitors can't make it — I think that this is all of us" said Janice.

"Okay, let's start" said George. "Now I am well aware that we all have concerns about the new computer system. Not just the system itself, but also what it means in terms of our work practices. As most of you know I've been on a 'Computer Day' with other Team Managers to find out about the system. I want to share with you what I learnt on that day."

Bill Thurlow interrupted, "How about asking us if we want it in the first place?"

"Bill, of course I am interested in your view and the views of all the Team. And so is the Clinical Director" replied George. "The computer system", he continued, "is called the Patient Information and Administrative System; PIAS for short. All Community Teams throughout the district will have a terminal in their Team Office. This is connected up to the Computer Centre at Community Headquarters. Each Team member will keep computer information on each patient they see. Information such as demographic data, diagnosis, reason for referral and so forth. You will have your own password and some information will only be accessible by you. Other information will be accessible by me, or other Team members.

Every time you see a patient you update the file — putting in information such as what you did – a wound dressing perhaps, how much time it took, what the travelling time was. In this way a complete record of, for example, nursing care given, can be built up. Say we are talking about a post-operative patient — a physiotherapist may also be seeing the patient. You can access her file and find out exactly when she visited and for what purpose."

"What's the point of that? — Physiotherapists already keep written records which are updated at each patient contact" interjected Ann.

"So do Nurses" added Betty.

"Well, two reasons" replied George. "Firstly you can find out what each other is doing more easily. Secondly, and more controversially, it's about General Practitioner fund-holding. Eighty per cent of our GPs are now fund-holders. We are a provider unit, they are responsible for purchasing our services for their patients. At the moment we have little idea what it costs to buy a course of physiotherapy for back-pain. By using the computer system, we can build up a picture of how many patients each of you see, where you see them and how long you see them for. Then we add in costs like office space and secretarial time, and we can tell GP fund-holders exactly how much a service costs, and how efficient the service is."

Bill looked as though he was about to explode. "I see, it's all about money. It's about buying and selling health care. In my opinion the whole purchaser/provider nonsense is just about turning health care into a business. This fancy computer isn't to help us — it's to help the Clinical Director say how much we cost. It stinks!"

"Any minute now he'll tell us about how he's deeply committed to the NHS", thought George.

"I'm deeply committed to the NHS", shouted Bill, "and I feel we should vigorously oppose anything which makes the NHS reforms easier to put in place."

George looked at Bill. "I don't think this is the appropriate arena to air your feelings about the politics of the NHS reforms. Whether you approve of the changes is neither here nor there. We would be getting the computer system anyway."

Ann tried to calm things down, "We've discussed all this before Bill. Let's try to stay focused on the topic of the computer system itself, not the reasons that are behind us getting it. I'm concerned about the extra work. Instead of having laboriously complete written records about patients we will have to laboriously complete written records and computer records. I personally didn't become a physiotherapist to sit all day in front of a computer."

"I agree", said Betty, "Community Nurses have enough to do without an administrative workload."

"I've got an Occupational Therapist friend in Wales who uses PIAS, who says you have to fill in a lot of information which is irrelevant to

Occupational Therapy" volunteered Louise.

George managed to quieten them down.

"The IT Manager, John Ireland, assures me that there will be very little extra work. Each Team member carries something like a plastic board with bar-codes on and a light pen. It will be just like the checkout at Sainsbury's. You swipe a bar-code — for example 'giving an injection' and then swipe a code for time taken, place seen etc. At the end of the day you simply download the light pen and all your records will be automatically updated. Of course, we need to ensure that all possible activities are included and that you don't have to be bothered with irrelevant information. We can talk to the IT Manager about that. You, and I, as Team Manager will be able to monitor exactly all your given activity for any given day."

A hubbub of noise broke out. Everyone was talking at once, everyone was angry. Betty got to her feet, "I've been a District Nurse for over twenty years and you can stand there and tell me that my job is nothing but a set of bar-codes! My God! George, before you tell me any more just remember that you used to be a Clinical Nurse before you were a Manager. If nursing is just a matter of giving injections, dressing wounds and carrying out tasks then I feel I've wasted my time all these years. Is that how Senior Management sees us? Automatons who go around sticking needles into people and putting bandages on? What about the need to talk to people, counsel them. Educating them and their families. There's more to dressing a wound than slapping on a plaster! You have to look for signs of healing, signs of infection. You assess how the wound affects their mobility and find out what the patient is worried about but I suppose all that counts for nothing!"

Bill took up the debate.

"I entirely agree", began Bill, "and in my job it's even less task-orientated. Psychiatric nursing is all about the quality of relationship you build with the patient and his family — how do you bar-code that?"

George's comments about it being "just like the checkout at Sains-bury's" had really angered Bill. The last person he would compare him-self to was a checkout operative in a supermarket.

"Bill, it's not about quality, it's about collecting quantitative data. That doesn't mean managers aren't interested in quality, we are. We have to know the quantitative stuff to run an effective service" said George. Really he could have guessed they'd be up in arms about quality.

"I don't believe you! It's not the quality you want, it's about how many patients you see, how quickly you do things. Cram as many pa-tients into the day as possible — never mind the uselessness of what you are doing. It's an insult to us as professionals. Talk about Big Brother is watching you." Bill stared truculently around the room.

"Calm down Bill", replied George, "why don't we try and look at some of the advantages of the computer system."

"I haven't finished." Bill was shouting now. "Half the time we spend wouldn't even show up on the computer. What about the ten phone calls trying to get through to Social Services? And being asked to hold for ages and then getting through to the wrong person? I waste hours on the phone every week. If you are going to expect to know exactly what I'm doing, and that I'm working 100% of the working day you'll need to know that!"

"Shut-up Bill" snapped George. "As for that, time on the phone can easily be accommodated, and we can record whether contact was successfully made or not. Managers aren't stupid you know."

"Yes, shut-up Bill, I can't understand what George is saying if you are going to shout all the time" said Louise, the Occupational Therapist.

"Look" continued George. "With the computer you can call up all sorts of useful information at the touch of a button. You can generate a list of your patients, or a list of other professionals who have contact with your patients."

"That's assuming we can work out how to use the computer in the first place" interrupted Betty.

George sighed, "Let me finish Betty, I'll talk about training needs later. You can find out if your patient has previously been seen by a member of this Team, and why. You could get the computer to flag up any patient who hasn't been seen for a while and needs to be discharged or visited."

"I can see all that", said Louise, "and I agree it would be useful. What I'm worried about is that it will create a state of intense rivalry within the Team. Who can see most patients: do Occupational Therapists see more patients than nurses and vice versa? Also, if a whole range of people have access to patient information, how do we maintain confidentiality?"

Bill was off again. "Yes, that's another thing, confidentiality. Maud Brain, the Clinical Psychologist, says she doesn't want her patient records being made accessible to all Team members. After all, if Betty goes round to deal with somebody's varicose ulcers why should she know that the person is receiving psychological help? Unless the patient wants Betty to know, of course. In a rural area like this, confidentiality is a big issue. And I feel the same. Should the Team always know if a CPN is involved?"

Louise had had previous arguments with Bill about this. "There's no need for you people who work in Mental Health to be so precious about confidentiality. All patient information is confidential. A patient might not want a CPN to know that he or she is seeing an Occupational Therapist."

Bill laughed nastily. "Well I certainly wouldn't want to admit to anyone that I was seeing an OT."

Louise and Bill looked set to embark on arguments of long standing as to the relative merits of their respective professions.

"Oh shut-up you two!" shouted Ann. "I want to hear what George says."

George gave Ann a grateful look. "We do need to talk more about all these issues, and in particular the Data Protection Act . . . "

". . . You bet we need to talk about more" shouted Bill, "but I'm not talking now. Some of us have got work to do. Real work, not a load of old guff about how brilliant computers are." Bill began to gather his things together.

Sharon, the nursing assistant spoke for the first time. "I'm really interested in computers. My boyfriend is doing a degree in computer science and he's been telling me some of the things computers can do these days. I'm fed-up with never knowing what's going on with the patients I visit. I'll be able to learn more about what happens to patients when the computer comes."

"Thank you Sharon. I'm glad to see at least one member of the Team can see something positive in all this" said George. "Now, I have to go, but I'd like you all to think about what's been said today, positive things as well as criticisms. We will discuss it further soon."

As George left the meeting room he could hear Bill shouting excitedly.

"It's bloody marvellous isn't it. The Health Authority is £50 000 in overspend and they're spending money on this. Some computer man in a suit from London invents this system and makes thousands and thousands of pounds out of it — and I bet you he wouldn't know a patient if one jumped up and bit him on the nose!"

George was less than happy at the way in which the meeting had gone. He didn't feel he had handled it well. The more he tried to sell the benefits of the system, the more oppositional they had become. Except Sharon, and that was only because her boyfriend liked computers, he thought cynically. Perhaps he should have talked to them individually, or maybe got John Ireland down to explain it. He had felt quite confident after his computer away-a-day, but explaining it to others made him realize he knew less about it than he had thought. The main difficulty was that he wasn't sure he had really understood what they were upset about. And could he do anything about it if he knew?

5.2.2 The aftermath

Betty and Ann were doing a joint nursing/physiotherapy visit immediately after the meeting. They were to re-assess a man with multiple sclerosis who was wheelchair-bound and incontinent of urine. His wife was deeply unhappy about having to give up work to care for him.

He had two teenage sons — one of whom was getting into trouble at school for truancy. The case was obviously an important one for them to discuss, but they continued to discuss the computer system in the car on the way there.

"It really worries me Betty. Not just because of what it means in terms of the way the Health Service is changing — but how it may affect my job."

Ann was a single parent and had to juggle work with taking her children to and from school, getting them to the dentist etc. "It's hard enough as it is to fit everything in, but at least now, if I need to leave work early because of the kids, I can. If George is going to use the computer to monitor how much time I spend doing things he may put a stop to that. And I always have a long lunch hour on Thursdays to go to the bank and do the shopping at Sainsbury's. I know it's work-time, but I just can't face dragging the kids round the supermarket in the evening. I often do paperwork at home in the evening to catch up, I do get the work done. Also — if I have to go back to the Health Centre at the end of each day to update the computer that's an extra trip in the car. I normally pick up the kids from the childminders straight after my last visit."

"I remember when mine were little" said Betty. "I only worked part-time and my Mum looked after them. But it wasn't easy."

"Childcare costs me a fortune, Betty. A friend of mine in Canterbury told me they got a new computer system and that by five o'clock there was a queue of people waiting to use the terminal. She reckoned you sometimes waited an hour to get on the computer."

"Why don't employers realize that people like you, with kids to bring up on your own, are on a tight timetable?" sighed Betty.

"It's not fair is it? Single mums get all the blame for living on benefit and having delinquent kids but employers make it very difficult for us to work."

Ann sounded really worried. She couldn't afford to leave work any later and so have to pay extra childcare costs.

Betty was silent while she coaxed her elderly car up a steep hill. This completed, she was able to voice her own concerns.

"I'm worried about using the computer at all. I'm useless at anything like that — I can't even set the timer on the video. I know I won't be able to master it however much training they give me. I hate computers." Betty was worried that everyone would think her a fool if she couldn't use the computer.

"You see, Ann", she continued, "I know you youngsters can use them — they even have them in schools now — but in my day they weren't even invented. My son told me about a boy in his class who turned the switches off in the wrong order — and the whole machine broke down. He did thousands of pounds' worth of damage just by turning a switch! What if I did that? I'd probably get the sack."

"Sometimes I wish I'd never joined the Health Service" said Ann, "they just won't leave us alone. Look, here we are, and we haven't even thought about the patient."

Bill and Sharon had a cup of coffee together before going home. "I know I'm only the nursing assistant", said Sharon, "but I can't see what all the fuss is about, we did a lot of stuff with computers when I was doing NVQs at college. I really enjoyed it."

"It's not the technology that bothers me" said Bill. "It's all the hidden agendas behind it. You mark my words — the Clinical Director can look at the statistics and say Nurse X did an average of six visits a morning. But Nurse Y in a different team did an average of ten visits. He can say if Nurse Y can do ten visits why can't Nurse X? They could use this information to cut nursing posts. That's bad for us, and bad for patients."

"Maybe they will say Nurse Y is doing too many visits. They could use the information to justify more posts couldn't they?" asked Sharon.

"Don't be naive! You want to do your general nurse training when you've finished your NVQs don't you?" asked Bill.

"Yes I do . . . but what's that got to do with it?"

"Less jobs, less nurses, less training places for nurses. No training place for you. Anyway — I'd better be going — got to get my work done or it will be my job being cut." Bill sounded no less furious now than he had when challenging George. He didn't seriously believe his job was at risk, but did believe that jobs might be at risk if people like him didn't stand up to managers. And he did, after all, have a wife and kids to support.

George had returned to his office when Bill left the building. He watched Bill walk across the car park and get into his car. He then returned to his desk and his cup of nearly-cold coffee. He was writing a list. This is what he wrote:

1. Get IT Manager down.
2. Confidentiality — Data Protection Act.
3. Training needs.
4. Visit to see computer in operation?
5. Get Semtex to blow up computer!

5.3 What can we learn?

What can we learn from the reactions of the Community Team to the proposed computer system? As we have seen, several members of the Team were markedly unenthusiastic about it. George, the Manager, was left wondering whether he really understood what their fears and problems were.

Perhaps George could have tackled the problem differently. He has allowed a situation to develop whereby he is caught between the demands of senior management and the fears of his staff. By maintaining secrecy (albeit unsuccessfully) about the coming computer system he has merely fostered mistrust and a feeling of helplessness in his staff. Had he taken them into his confidence before the away-a-day he might well have had some useful ideas about staff concerns to take to that meeting with him. He could, perhaps, have asked a member of the Team to work with him on the computer system implementation or even delegate much of the responsibility to that person. The way in which he did handle the issue left the Team without any sense of ownership of the system and thus resentful and oppositional before they had even heard the facts.

Let us now examine in more detail the negative reactions of the individual Team members, look at the general reasons why people react to proposed change in ways such as this and how it informs professional practice for software engineers.

5.3.1 Group polarization

George tries to outline to the Team the advantages of the system. This results in group polarization — where a group of people will take up a more extreme position than they would as individuals, in the face of somebody trying to alter their attitudes. Telling people something is good which they already think is bad rarely shifts attitudes in the desired direction!

Sharon's support for George and the system only infuriates Bill and Betty all the more.

As a group they have concerns about the introduction of the computer system — another change to cope with, more stress, a manifestation of the NHS reforms. As individuals they also have concerns relating to their own situations.

5.3.2 Technophobia

Betty Hislop — the District Nurse — suffers from fear of technology. She feels threatened by the idea of having to learn a new and possibly difficult set of skills. It is often the case that as people grow older they become less confident in their abilities to learn new skills, despite the fact that people can and do learn new things throughout their lives. It is less a case of inability than lack of confidence — fear of exposing yourself to others as foolish or stupid. Betty not only fears that she will be seen as incompetent but also fears that she will make some catastrophic blunder. It should be noted that fear of technology is not confined to older adults and none of us relish the prospect of appearing a fool.

5.3.3 Change in work patterns

Ann is worried about the impact of the computer system on the way she manages to fit work around the demands of her young children. She thinks that if George can tell at the touch of a button how much work she is doing her current coping strategy for balancing home and work will be threatened. There is, of course, no objective evidence or likelihood that George would use the computer in this way. The threat lies in Ann's fear that he might — or, if not George, then perhaps the Clinical Director might do so.

Bill's comment is "talk about Big Brother is watching you!". Ann also says people will be queuing up to use the computer terminal every evening which will put her under even more time pressure. Time pressure is one of the biggest sources of strain for Ann and whilst this problem may have an easy solution, her current concern is the potential threat.

5.3.4 Threat to professional status

Betty and Bill talk of their job being reduced to a set of bar-codes. The threat in this case is to their self-esteem and feelings of self-worth. They perceive their jobs as requiring a high level of interpersonal skill, experience and maturity. As these things cannot be measured quickly and easily, the data they will collect focuses by necessity on those aspects of their jobs which can be measured. By making their jobs appear less complex the computer system is perceived, in some way, as de-skilling and downgrading them.

5.3.5 Fears of competition

Louise, the Occupational Therapist, says that the computer will create rivalry: because information is so easily accessible managers can make comparisons between different members of the Team without taking into account the different types of clinical problems they are engaged with. The Clinical Director could unreasonably compare one team with another. Whenever a group of people have comparisons made about their respective work performance there is always the threat one might be found wanting in relation to others.

5.3.6 Fears of redundancy

Bill develops this argument further. He is worried that the information derived from the computer could be used to cut jobs. If all primary health teams are compared and one team found to see significantly more patients it is easy to conclude that this is the best-performing team. Similarly, if one nurse in one location sees as many patients as two nurses in another location it might be argued that two nurses are not needed in the second location. This ignores such considerations as longer travelling times, greater social deprivation or sicker patients. Bill has chosen to forget that many managers who use information are capable of interpreting the data sensitively and intelligently.

5.3.7 Loss of confidentiality and control

It is Louise who raises the issue of confidentiality, which is, of course, a proper concern for anyone who collects information about people. But the real issue for Louise, Bill and Maud Brain, the Psychologist, is a concern about who owns the data. If the data can be accessed by George, the Clinical Director and their colleagues their ownership of the data is called into question. They fear they will lose control over the information they keep on their patients.

The issue of "ownership" is raised under the guise of "confidentiality". Part of George's confusion about the problems for the Team with the computer results from this common tendency of problems raised being disguised as different problems. There is one key issue underpinning all the concerns of the Team, both global, shared concerns and private worries. That is the notion of threat. The Team, already under stress from other sources, are vulnerable to perceiving threatening consequences from the introduction of the computer system. These threats are not necessarily realistic, some arise from misconceptions and lack of understanding about the uses and limitations of information technology.

5.4 Stress

Stress has been mentioned as an important determinant of the group's reactions to the new system. So what is stress? Stress is defined as any stimulus which an individual perceives as taxing his or her coping resources. Stress is not necessarily bad, in fact it motivates us to meet new challenges and responsibilities and to find novel and creative ways to solve problems. Without stress there can be little real job satisfaction or sense of personal mastery.

Stress has to be met using a variety of strategies — such as seeking information, taking problem-solving action or thinking about the problem in a different way. These strategies may vary between individuals and the same individual may meet stress at different times by activating different strategies. Successfully finding a strategy to cope with stress leads to feelings of mastery and personal effectiveness.

Sometimes people fail to find effective ways of dealing with stress. When stressful stimuli are beyond the coping resources of the individual they experience strain, hopelessness and anxiety. This, in its turn, makes the generation of effective new strategies less likely; leading to a cycle of failure to cope and further stress. When people have been under prolonged stress for a considerable period of time they may find that their coping resources are exhausted. Something like a new computer system can be the straw that breaks the camel's back.

Whether a stimulus (such as the impending arrival of a computer system) is perceived as stressful or not varies in relation to the predictability of the stressor, the degree to which it is perceived as threatening, the novelty of the stressor (have we met this situation before?) and the amount of time pressure we are under. A further determinant of our ability to cope with stress is our perceived control over the situation. In the example of the Community Health Team, the people who will use the system perceive themselves as having no control over its introduction. The situation is likely to be a novel one for most of them, they are already under time pressure and they cannot predict what it will be like actually using the system. This is an addition to the feelings of some Team members that the computer is being introduced to facilitate changes in the NHS to which they may be opposed.

5.4.1 Perceived threat

Things are experienced as stressful when they are perceived as carrying threat. The key word here is *perceived*. Whether or not a stimulus is perceived as threatening depends on the interpretation that is made of the stimulus. Any stimulus can be interpreted in a number of ways. If, for example, you were woken by a loud crash in the kitchen in the middle of the night your reaction would depend on your interpretation of the event. If you thought it was your teenage son coming in late from a party you may react with anger. If you believed that the cat had knocked over a milk-bottle you might ignore it completely. Should you appraise the noise as being due to a burglar entering the house you would react with fear. The emotion aroused depends on your interpretation of what, in each case, is the same event. Some of us are more prone to interpret situations as being threatening when under existing stress.

Betty perceived the computer system would threaten her self-esteem because of her self-appraisal of herself as being no good with technology. Ann perceived that the computer system would threaten her ability to combine work and home commitments. Bill perceived that the breaking down of his job into easily measurable components would reduce his job complexity in his own eyes and the eyes of others. Louise perceived that professional rivalry would result from the ease with which information could be obtained. The interpretations these individuals made were not the only interpretations which could have been made, and are not necessarily the interpretations which reflect most realistically the effect which the computer system might have.

5.4.2 Cooperation

How does this help the software engineer? Perhaps the most important point is that however good the system is there may be problems related to getting people to use it. The answer to these problems often does not lie in altering the system itself, but working with others to be aware of and reduce the perceived threat. You can only do this if you understand the organization you are working with. There are no magic solutions to the problems individuals have with using a new computer system, but people do like to feel consulted, that they have had a part in deciding what data will be collected and how. People do not like change and threat is often implicit in change. The need for change may imply existing methods are not satisfactory — and thus be construed as criticism. Extolling the virtues of a system to people who are opposed often results in group polarization and a hardening of attitudes. Within a group of individuals confronted with a new task, there will always be global shared concerns and private worries. In extreme cases, something like a new computer system can act as a catalyst to bring simmering discontent to group awareness — pity the poor user indeed!

It is important, however time-consuming, that a representative sample of users are consulted about the system. Only by doing this, will users become actively involved and develop any sense of ownership towards the system. Self-esteem in the workplace can always be lowered by ignoring workers' views and always be raised by asking for their help. People are nearly always flattered and pleased by the opportunity to describe their job to an outsider.

As a software engineer you can increase your credibility to both users and purchasers by your ability to engage sensitively and creatively with the types of problem outlined in this chapter. Just because the solutions may not lie in your hands does not mean that they are not your concern.

About the author

Hilary Husband is a clinical psychologist working for the Norfolk Mental Health Trust, and has been a victim of software engineers. Though she suspects that a suit is the adult equivalent of a comfort blanket, she has no strong opinions about the software engineer's sartorial choice. She does, however, have much sympathy with George Bernard Shaw's observation in the *Doctor's Dilemma* that "All professions are conspiracies against the laity".

Further reading

Arroba T. and James K. (1992), *Pressure at Work*, McGraw-Hill.
Curtis S. and Curtis B. (1994), *Behaviour at Work*, Pitman.
Handy C. (1989), *The Age of Unreason*, Arrow.
Hunt J. (1992), *Managing People at Work*, McGraw-Hill.

SIX

THE PERILS OF FREELANCING
BY WENDY STOKES

6.1 Introduction

There are some stages of a career in Information Technology when the appeal of freelance work will call into question loyalty to your company's goals, promotion prospects and pay structure. Although the goldrush of the 1980s has come to an end, there is still freelance work for those who want its ambivalent rewards. These will be people who have a history of permanent employment and want to taste something different; freelancing is inadvisable, and generally inaccessible, for college-leavers.

The joys of being only temporarily attached are well known and accessible to the imagination of any poor soul updating documentation, whose next pay-rise is a year away. However, not all the perils are immediately apparent. There is the fear of getting the first contract but never getting another. Fair enough, it is a reasonable worry and anyone who could not handle that happening should beware. However, even if contracts flow one from another and agencies pay up on time, there are factors of which the "sussed" operator should be aware. These fall into three categories: the first category comprises dangers to your professional development, the second of dangers to your personal development, and the third is a broad category comprising the sorts of things that any sane human being would wish to avoid.

6.2 Dangers to your professional development

First things first. How can a job endanger your professional development? Well, there is the risk of getting locked into an out-dated speciality. The company has bought you in to perform something that you already know how to do and they may well want you to go on doing it. And on, and on. This leads to dangers two, three and four. Since you are already doing what your employers want you to do you may not receive much training in new technical skills. Similarly, you are unlikely to receive guidance on career development, training for promotion or management, or training in inter-personal skills. As a result of being locked into a company and a skill you run the risk of getting out of touch with the profession outside of your company. However, this is not compensated for by involvement with your employer: since your role in the company is limited and temporary you will probably be excluded from meetings. This might sound like a bonus until you realize that it is through those meetings that people keep track of what is going on, in terms of both planning and relationships. Access to this sort of knowledge could be one of your resources to combat the final danger: that of becoming dependent on a company without even the minimal statutory protection enjoyed by permanent staff.

Another thing to consider is your relationship to the product on which you are working. In this context you are just like any other employee and you have no rights over it: whatever you produce belongs to the company for which you are working. This will have been stitched up in the series of contracts existing between you, your agency and the client company. There may be circumstances in which you own, or want to own, the product: this brings you to the problem of intellectual property rights, which requires skilled legal advice and is dealt with elsewhere in this volume. As a freelance you may have a more distant relationship to the object of your labours than permanent staff: this may or may not trouble you, but is worth bearing in mind.

6.3 Dangers to your personal development

Perhaps you can circumvent all those pitfalls. In which case, consider our second category: dangers to your personal development. For starters, you may find yourself always taking work, however tired you are and however horrid the job, because you are always anxious about the possibility of those empty weeks with no invoices to submit. You may find yourself taking work in dreadful places, thereby compromising your private life, or taking work for dreadful companies, thereby compromising your peace of mind. To ensure that you have work, and some choice about where and what it is, you will read the computer press, a danger in itself. These papers are free once you are on the relevant mailing lists (easily achieved by stealing the form from someone else's copy; offices where freelances work are always littered with them), and so they should be. No-one should have to pay to read such mind-numbing articles — especially since advertisers have already paid a lot of money to place their vacancies on the back pages.

6.4 Dangers unique to the world of the IT freelance

6.4.1 Agents

If you are strong enough to remain steadfast to your goal of a blue-chip company located near to a gym, a good pub and Sainsbury's, you may yet baulk at some perils unique to the position of the IT freelance. You will have to spend time with agents, both while looking for work and, once working, every time you need to renew your contract and negotiate a rate review. Some agents even feel compelled to take you out for a drink once in a while to jolly you along and pump you for information about the company. None of this is pleasant. Agents may, individually and in their private lives, be decent people, but their work consists in wheeling, dealing, wheedling, and a few other crocodilian activities. You, on the other hand, are one of a flock of pet geese laying the golden eggs which are financing your agent's inflated lifestyle. This does not feel good and excessive interaction with agents is best avoided.

A particularly frightening characteristic possessed by some agents is a confidence in your skills which far outstrips anything appearing on your CV, however optimistic that document might be. This can lead you into the nightmare of feeling obliged to lie about what you can do, because the agent has already lied on your behalf. This will entail spending dreadful nights either trying to learn things or wondering when you are going to be found out.

6.4.2 Innocence

Moving away from agents and developing a point made earlier, as the innocent Candide of the IT department you may well get caught in the crossfire of company politics that you don't understand and that no-one bothers to explain. Here is a personal anecdote of what this can lead to. I once spent three months cheerfully designing, writing and testing an add-on to a personnel system that would handle the company's statutory sick pay obligations. While doing this I was supervised by Eddie, who had interviewed and employed me. Implementation loomed. One morning I was called into the office of a chap I had seen wandering around the department. He turned out to be Eddie's boss who was very put out by young Ed's empire building (which comprised me and my subsystem) and was putting a stop to it by having the whole thing re-specified, redesigned and rewritten. You can imagine how distressed I was when I tell you that I had already written the documentation! One thing of which you can be sure: whatever happens, once you are gone the manager will get the credit and you will get the blame.

6.5 Some extra worries — or maybe not!

The final section in this catalogue of discouragement comprises some points, inherent to the nature of freelancing, which are ambivalent. There are circumstances in which these points might be construed as disappointments, and others where they might be benefits.

6.5.1 Temporariness

First, a function of your temporariness: just when you have got to know the system it is time to move on. While this might seem to be a waste of the knowledge and experience you have accumulated, it is not rare for familiarity to breed mistrust; your position of illumination may include the knowledge that you do not want to be there when the whole thing falls apart — and as a freelance you don't have to be.

6.5.2 Specialization

Second, a function of your specialization: as someone brought in to perform a more or less specific task you do not get to understand the entire vision or perceive the full lifecycle of the project. Again a mixed blessing, rather depending on the quality of the operation. It is worth noting that few amongst permanent staff get to see the whole picture, and that in many cases not even Rip van Winkle would see completion.

6.5.3 Control

Third: as someone whose job description is fairly tightly drawn you have little control over where the project is going (unless you have been brought in to direct it, in which case your responsibility is awesome, especially in the light of the potential for exclusion and scapegoating outlined above). This can cause either intense frustration or giddy light-headedness, depending upon how valuable you judge the project to be and how seriously you take your career.

6.6 Protecting yourself

Sounding rather grim? Do not despair. There are points of light shining through this pall of gloom: there are things you can do to protect yourself. Here are two groups of strategies. Those in the first group are sensible and practical and should be pursued with maturity and judgement. Those in the second require skills of positioning, manipulation and negotiation, which you should be well on the way to acquiring if you have come back for your second and third contract.

6.6.1 Practical things

Accountants

First things first. Get an accountant through recommendation or through the Yellow Pages who is properly qualified and specializes in small businesses. Friends may offer to do your books, but it is hard to get forceful with them when they forget to tell you things or don't get your books done in time because their child, your god-daughter, is teething. On the other hand, it is exciting and reassuring to have an accountant who is skilfully negotiating company mergers, but will they really place due importance on your VAT return? Next, get a limited company. You will have to do it or agencies will not touch you. Companies exist which do all the messy stuff of setting up the legal framework of other companies just to sell them on to people like you, so buy one off the shelf, with the silliest name going!

CVs

I am assuming that you have already prepared a CV while convincing yourself that you need to leave your present employer. If not, are you really serious about this? Do it now. Make it concise and informative. This is relevant because you are about to select some agencies and hand over your CV. Many agencies send this document, unaltered, out to clients, so be sure about what it says. Once you are ready to look for work, scan the press and contact agencies. Agencies which attempt to provide a service to their clients will interview you before sending out your CV and your sweet self. Remember that the agency's first loyalty is to itself and its second to the clients who pay the bills; you come a very poor third. You will only ever know what the agency is prepared to pay you for your services to their client; you will never know what the client pays the agency and therefore how large the agency's cut is. Some clients set a ceiling as part of their contract with the agency. These are usually very large clients which do not pay particularly well anyway, offering status and a degree of job security instead.

Agencies

Agencies may provide services for you, putting you in touch with accountants or helping you with interview technique, for example, or they may do nothing at all. There is no need for you to commit yourself to the first agency that is nice to you, or to any agency at all until one comes up with a job that you want — although you may find that life is simpler if you confine your phone calls and your CV to a selection of three or four agencies whose representatives have soothing telephone manners. Even once you have a contract, your commitment to the agency need last only as long as that job.

However efficient and caring an agency is, or otherwise, they all have entrenched habits of secrecy. This means that they will rarely tell you which clients have been sent your CV, or even which client you are about to go to for an interview. Agents accompany you to your interviews and may sometimes tell you where you are going en route. This is because agencies are ranged against each other in vicious competition and do not want you to tell any other agency that this or that company is looking for this or that staff. Since it is likely that you will be looking for work through more than one agency this can cause problems and embarrassment. I once went for an interview at a company which, it turned out, had received my CV from seven different agencies. After the interview I was taken aside and informed, in a whisper, that the company would like to take me, but not through the agency that had brought me for interview. They would like to employ me through another one which was offering my services more cheaply.

Insurance

Once you have started work you need to think about replacing for yourself all the things that you (may) have taken for granted while in permanent employment. High on this list is a pension plan, followed closely by insurance to cover your commitments if you are ill or injured, and a strategy to cope with periods of unemployment. For the first two you need the advice of an independent expert allied to a sensible assessment of your needs and expectations: The third depends entirely on you. Some people will save to cover for this eventuality, some will not. Some people will fill in gaps with temporary work in other sectors, others will read books or play golf. How you plan to deal with it is up to you, the important thing is that you have thought it through at the outset.

6.6.2 Imaginative things

Socializing

Moving along to our second group of strategies involving skills of positioning, manipulation and negotiation, the first point that must be made is painful but important: do not hang out exclusively with other freelances; socialize with the permanent staff. You cannot learn what is going on by only mixing with other people who don't know. This may not be such a wrench as it sounds: the glamour of freelancing and freelancers is pretty thin, they are much the same people doing much the same things as in your old department. The faces may change, the conversations about football and EastEnders rarely do. If you follow this suggestion the other strategies will be less daunting than they appear. These are to insinuate yourself onto training courses at any opportunity, on any pretext, however irrelevant they appear in the short term. Then to insinuate yourself into the company. Ideally people should forget for periods of time that you are not one of them. This way you get to be both informed and consulted.

Dress for success

Whilst doing all of the above you should dress for success. Quickly and carefully assess the dress code and practice of your new employer and calculate for yourself a style which is authoritative but one-of-us. You want to avoid eccentricities which will call into question either your ability or your suitability. Hitting the right note can guarantee that people will take you seriously — and leave you alone — while you are desperately finding out what you are meant to be doing.

Pragmatism

This desperation, which often ensues when facing the reality of a new contract, can be mitigated by consistent pragmatism: use existing code and designs, yours or other people's, whenever you can — and take particularly useful bits with you when you leave; steal or photocopy manuals; steal favours — often when you have hit a wall of incomprehension there is someone who would love to help you out if approached appropriately. Flattery usually works. If you have established yourself as a decent sort of person through these recommended manoeuvres, you can afford to relax a bit and admit to weaknesses — as a last resort. People like to offer support and help, as long as it neither inconveniences them nor exposes them to any risk.

6.7 So why do it?

Taking note of all this, why does anyone do it? The final answer is always a personal one, however, it will contain the following factors, variously weighted.

Money. It pays well, although rarely as well as our wildest dreams, and does permit a certain flexibility about when to work and how much to work.

Movement. The possibility of moving on is ever-present, therefore even if you don't change jobs every three months, you are constantly choosing to be where you are. This is empowering and can make tedium tolerable.

Choice. By working in different environments you get to know what you prefer and can exercise educated choice about work. Careful selection of work can provide you with desirable skills and experience, which can counter some of the adverse effects listed above.

Choosing to work freelance is often part of a greater, not always articulated, plan. It may be straightforwardly financial: to make as much money as possible in a period of time in order to do something specific. It may be tactical: minimal commitment to work for a period while your energies are focused elsewhere. It may be strategic: evidence of an adventurous and experimental approach to work. The trick is, as in any other field of endeavour, to know yourself, be aware of what you are doing, and realize when the time has come to get a proper job.

About the author

Wendy Stokes was a freelance programmer and analyst with large and powerful organizations for several years. She now lectures in politics and sociology. Regarding suits: for women in male-focused environments, wearing a comfortable suit — not an American power-dressing number — can produce a camouflage effect and simplify work relations. On the other hand, as an 'in-comer', a freelance has to adapt to the customs of the community; so whether to be suited or dungareed is not a free choice!

CHAPTER SEVEN

THE REPTILIAN WORLD OF SOFTWARE TEAMS

BY JOHN MADSEN

7.1 Introduction

You need teams to deliver useful software. You need teams with the right sort of people combining the right skills. While this assertion is both simple and obvious, forging the right team is often difficult. This chapter will help you to understand where you fit in a team, and how you can build the right teams to deliver successful software solutions. It will help you to build successful teams by addressing the following three issues:

1. The current state of the software development business and the historical background that has got us to where we are. This brief history of Information Technology describes why we need a particular type of team to deliver useful software. It also focuses on the myths and legends that permeate IT, the environment in which we are all working.
2. Classification systems — particularly ways of classifying people to see if they can help us to design ideal software teams.
3. Finally, having examined some people classifications and found them helpful, but not tailored to our needs, I will propose a simple classification model that will help software engineers to decide what they are, what they are best at, and what other types of people they will need in their teams.

7.2 A brief history of IT and software teams

IT is a young business, about half as old as the aerospace industry. It is so young that it still fits within a human lifespan. Despite its youth IT has now been around long enough to have accumulated a past, together with myths, legends, customs, practices and stereotypes. We need to understand the evolution of IT, and its accumulated past to appreciate why we need teams and why building the right teams is both important and difficult. I will define four ages of IT:

1. Prehistory
2. The Dark Ages
3. The Industrial Revolution
4. The Post Modern Era

7.2.1 Prehistory

That long period BC (Before Computers). Somehow the human race struggled on, not knowing what it was missing. There were noble attempts to start the industry by Babbage and Hollerith, but generally speaking, the hardware was inadequate. There were no software teams because there was no software. The Second World War and cryptography provided just the right catalyst and Turing ushered in . . .

7.2.2 The Dark Ages

. . . Colossus, and von Neumann (or someone else) invented the stored program computer. People who played with computers were "programmers". Theirs was a mystical black art. The rest of the world neither knew nor cared what they did, or how they did it. Programmers were alchemists. There were no methods or standards or agreed ways of doing things. Programmers were left to get on with it. Bizarre dress codes were a necessary part of preserving the computing mythology. Ancient wizards wore flowing multicoloured robes and pointed hats and carried a book of spells in a strange tongue as a symbol of their craft. Programmers affected casual clothes and an unkempt appearance. They wrote in esoteric languages in capital letters, on coding sheets. They carried reams of incomprehensible octal core dumps printed on green striped paper and mumbled incantations in assembler. In the Dark Ages there were no software teams, just solitary programmer-wizards who did everything themselves.

The Dark Ages were too much fun to last. Computing was forced out of its cosy niche, a victim of its own success. Computers began to be used for more than simply doing hard sums. They could be used to "automate", to "computerize", above all, to replace expensive clerical factories.

This was serious stuff, not to be treated lightly. If computers could be used in business, then computing had better clean up its act. Programmers would need to get professional. Software people became dissatisfied with their image. Users demanded demystification. Mistrust abounded. Software alchemists tried to formalize their mystic craft. Engineering looked like a good role model. After all, engineers were practical, logical, scientific people and computers were logical machines. The Dark Ages slipped into . . .

7.2.3 The Industrial Revolution

The Industrial Revolution marked the arrival of computing into the mainstream of organizations. It was characterized by:

◇ Belief that engineering principles could be used to turn the art into a science
◇ Increased specialization
◇ Methodologies
◇ Big projects (and long delivery timetables) and, of course,
◇ Big teams of software engineers.

Specialization

During the Industrial Revolution a Babel of languages developed. There were hundreds of programming languages to choose from, and dozens of tools to go with them. In addition to our old friends COBOL and FORTRAN, new productivity tools — Fourth Generation Languages — were offered as a panacea to improve productivity. Databases happened. There were "real" databases, hierarchical, network and even relational, together with re-badged file management systems which magically became databases. Brave attempts to automate the system development lifecycle included project planning support tools, Integrated Project Support Environments, Computer Assisted Software Engineering tools.

This rich variety of IT tools demanded an equally rich variety of specialists to use them. Where there were simple programmers before, terminology inflation yielded a bewildering variety of software engineers: systems analysts, analyst programmers, systems programmers, assembler programmers, 3GL programmers, developers, database engineers, communications specialists, human factors experts, systems integrators etc.

Methodologies

In addition to tools and specialists, the Industrial Revolution spawned methodologies with a vengeance. Methodologies for all seasons evolved towards today's rich and varied menu. As with standards, the nice thing about methodologies is that there are so many to choose from. There are methodologies to tackle problems that IT didn't know it had. The following list of generic methodology types may be exhausting, but it is not exhaustive: business analysis, systems analysis and design, application design, application development, systems integration, project planning and control, human–computer interface, job design.

At their best, methodologies provide a valuable formalization of common sense. They give us a standard way of approaching problems with some guarantees that our solution is complete and workable (although not necessarily ideal). At their worst, methodologies provide no more than safe, reassuring rituals for the software engineer. Unfortunately such purposeless ritual behaviour, in the absence of common sense, rarely leads to useful business solutions, although it does give the software engineer some displacement activity to fill the void. Whoops! Steady on. Although I am a methodology anarchist this chapter is not supposed to be a diatribe against methodological excesses.

The rich variety of tools, techniques and methodologies spawned during the Industrial Revolution means that we need teams of specialists to deliver IT solutions. There is too much variety for the solitary Dark Age programmer-wizard to cope with. Industrialized software factories worked on the assumption that we could tackle major projects by using teams of software engineers. There were Systems Analyst teams, Programming teams, Testing teams, Implementation teams, Database teams etc.

Methodology-rich, "waterfall" projects in which IT professionals identified separate stages of development have largely failed to deliver useful systems. The type of project plan illustrated in Fig. 7.1 simply does not fit the reality of the system lifecycle. It inevitably leads to systems which are not what the customer expected and which have no hope of meeting requirements, because business needs change over time.

These waterfall models imply some unfortunate untruths. First, it isn't a waterfall at all, it is an uphill struggle. The model implies that systems get finished. In reality, the only stable system is a dead one. Real systems that get used are in perpetual evolution. An alternate and more useful model is the spiral lifecycle.

Figure 7.2 illustrates the cyclic nature of software development. It shows that there is a continuous process of homing in on an often changing requirement with points of stability where the successful software team must deliver part solutions so that the customer can reap early

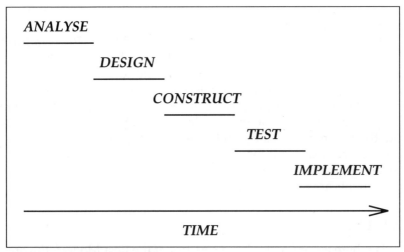

Figure 7.1 A waterfall project

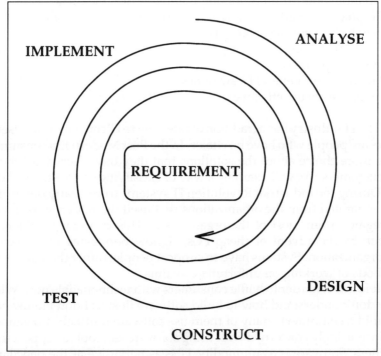

Figure 7.2 A software development spiral

benefits from the system. The spiral model implies that big, inflexible waterfall projects are doomed from the start.

The Industrial Revolution was a boom period for IT. Projects during this period were typically big. They employed a lot of specialists, organized into large teams, cost a lot of money and took a long time. While this was all good for software engineers, it was not always useful for customers. Big projects and big teams introduced new problems. Projects develop their own inertia and are difficult to steer or stop. They also grow their own bureaucracy and generate enormous internal communications overheads. All too often big projects run over cost and either miss the original requirements or take so long to deliver that the original requirements are no longer relevant.

7.2.4 The Post Modern era

This is where we are now. Characteristics of the Post Modern Era are:

◇ Customer choice
◇ No more opportunities for automating clerical factories
◇ Emphasis on building systems to support people at work
◇ Few technological constraints
◇ Focus on solving business problems, or even using IT to re-engineer business processes
◇ Much greater general IT awareness
◇ Available cheap, effective packaged software.

The IT industry has a tradition of referring to IT consumers as 'users'. Users are people who have no choice. In the Post Modern Era consumers have more choice about the solutions that they buy. Users with choice are customers. We will examine a way of classifying IT consumers later.

During the Industrial Revolution IT systems were clearly delineated and separated from the organizations that used them. Computers were segregated from most of the organization. This is no longer the case. Driven by the advent of cheap PCs, IT now permeates all corners of the organization. Systems have to support people, rather than imposing methods of working on unfortunate victims.

It is much harder to baffle consumers with technobabble now. While they don't understand how to build software (just as I don't know how to build a computer), many of them use software routinely. Consumers are increasingly concerned with using software as a tool to support their business. Software is a commodity. IT is as pervasive as the pencil and paper. It only has credibility as a tool to contribute towards the business objectives of an enterprise (or, in the case of games, as a means of filling leisure time).

Today, the role of the software engineer in mainstream IT is to provide IT-assisted solutions to business problems by:

◇ Doing things faster
◇ Doing things differently
◇ Doing things that were impractical before
◇ Doing things more competitively.

Software teams need to be small and quick and efficient in order to survive in the competitive Post Modern environment. In my (biased) opinion Rapid Application Development, through various forms of prototyping (Rapid Iterative Prototyping or Evolutionary Prototyping) offers the best chance of delivering effective custom IT solutions. We cannot afford the luxury of large dinosaur project teams peopled by narrow specialists.

There are plenty of tools, techniques, methodologies and software packages to address most business problems. Processing power is not usually a limiting factor (although we can always use more of it). The problem in the Post Modern era is increasingly people-focused. You may be in the exciting and fortunate position to be able to do IT for its own sake, but the likelihood is that you will be required to use your talents to build solutions to real-world problems. It is no longer sufficient to simply design and build systems that work (although we still need to do this!). The software engineering team must identify business problems where IT can help, persuade customers to buy the solution, analyse, design and build the appropriate system, implement the system, and evolve the system to meet changes in the business.

In order to build successful software teams we need a better understanding of the types of software engineer that make up the ideal team. The starting point is to evolve a new classification for software engineering people.

7.3 Civilization through classification

Taxonomy is one valuable method that humans use to make sense of a complicated world. Stereotypes, pigeonholes, generalizations, categories and even clichés allow us to organize the world into manageable frames of reference. For example, in biology, Linnaean classification of organisms into kingdoms, phyla and species helped us to generalize about plants and animals and revealed patterns that led to our understanding of biological evolution. Mendeleyev classified the elements into the Periodic Table, and was able to predict the existence of undiscovered elements, and their likely behaviour from the patterns visible in the Table.

In the IT world, we are perpetually classifying information and data, by type (character, numeric . . .) by entity, attribute and relationship, by volatility, by process, by object. We classify qualifications, jobs, everything, because otherwise the world is too complex to comprehend or manipulate.

We extend classifications into human society. We describe people as being tall, short, fat, thin, male, female and so on. We apply our own personal systems of stereotyping to everyone we meet and use these instant classifications in our dealings with other people. One of my favourite classifications for people is a system called CODOT which was used to match people to jobs. It is a favourite, both because of the glorious range of occupations that it covered, and because it was central to my first programming job. CODOT stands for Classification of Occupations and Directory of Occupational Titles. Here are some specific examples for your entertainment:

001.10	Ministers of the Crown
479.60	Pest Control Operator
044.30	Computer Programmer
726.99	Other fettling, grinding (excluding machine tool) and polishing operations (metal)

The classification went even further to cover (for example) computer programmers who specialize in ALGOL — a Dark Age programming language. We could use a classification system like CODOT to define the occupational skills that we need to build our team. It is simple to decide that a particular solution requires (for example) a 4GL developer, a screen designer, a database designer and someone with experience of LANs, but this on its own will not necessarily give us an effective software engineering team.

The problem for software engineers is to understand how to classify both themselves and their colleagues, so that they can forge teams that will deliver IT solutions in the Post Modern era. We must find a way of defining the team characteristics that we need.

7.3.1 Hippocratic humours

Hippocrates recorded an early personality classification in about 400 BC. He theorized that personalities (or temperaments) were caused by different balances of body "humours" in the individual. He proposed the following relationships:

Body humour	Temperament	Behaviour
Blood	Sanguine	Confident, optimistic
Black bile	Melancholic	Depressed, prone to ill-founded fears
Bile	Choleric	Active, aggressive, irritable
Phlegm	Phlegmatic	Sluggish, apathetic

This model is not very useful for building teams. It describes different types of behaviour, but it doesn't tell us what the different types of people are good at, or how we should exploit their characteristics.

7.3.2 Belbin management team roles

Belbin and his colleagues used a combination of psychometric tests to relate observed team behaviour to specific psychological traits. The most significant traits were identified as:

◇ Intelligence
◇ Dominance
◇ Extroversion/Introversion
◇ Stability/Anxiety.

Belbin defined eight roles as being necessary or useful in team work. He describes the combination of personality traits for each role as summarized in Table 7.1.

Plants are rather mercurial creatures. They sulk a lot when their ideas are not adopted. Monitor evaluators are natural planners. They also punch holes in the Plant's more outrageous ideas. Company Workers just get on and do it. Resource Investigators provide boundary spanning for the team. Teamworkers bend over backwards to make sure that the team functions smoothly. Finally, Finishers do just that. They make sure that the team delivers something that is complete and workable.

According to Belbin the full range of types is essential to produce a balanced team. Of course, a team need not necessarily include eight or more people, but a smaller team requires that individuals adopt secondary roles in addition to their preferred primary role.

Belbin's classification provides an excellent basis for classifying software engineering team members. Similarly, in *The Mythical Man Month*, [Brooks, 1975] proposes a set of programming team roles, derived from an original idea by Harlan Mills. The Brooks model, although a little dated and missing the Post Modern requirement for the team to win business from consumers, has some interesting roles; particularly the support required for the "Surgeon" or chief programmer.

Table 7.1 Belbin's team roles

Role	Traits	Description
Chairman	Dominant Extrovert Stable	Focuses on objectives; establishes work roles and boundaries of others; concerned to use human resources effectively; clarifies and sets agendas; summarizes and makes decisions; not necessarily highly intelligent or creative; good listener and communicator.
Shaper	Anxious Dominant Extrovert	High nervous energy; full of enthusiasm and drive; continually looks for opportunities for action from discussion and ideas; heavily involved in the team's actions and successes; the task leader of the group.
Plant	Dominant High IQ Introvert	Produces creative ideas; has new insights concerned with basics not details; tends to criticize; switches off if ideas are rejected.
Monitor/ Evaluator	High IQ Stable Introvert	Objective and serious; analyses ideas, rather than generates them; skilled in assimilation and interpretation of data; may be least motivated but has sound judgement.
Company Worker	Stable Controlled	Practical organizer, concerned with order and feasibility; methodical, efficient and systematic; poor at handling novelty or lack of structure; does not value ideas and suggestions that are not task related; inflexible, but responds to direction.
Resource Investigator	Stable Dominant Extrovert	Friendly, sociable, enthusiastic and positive about ideas and suggestions; goes outside the team to seek ideas and information; enthusiasm may fade quickly; stimulated by others; keeps the team in touch with reality.
Teamworker	Stable Extrovert Low dominance	Sensitive to team feelings and emotions; popular and supportive; uncompetitive and dislikes friction; good listener and communicator; holds the team together.
Finisher	Anxious Introvert	Concerned with detail and order; worries over possible mistakes; imparts a permanent sense of urgency; tends to lose sight of main objective; gets bogged down in detail.

Unfortunately, both the Brooks model, with ten specialized team roles and Belbin's eight different generalized team roles are far too big for simple software engineers to cope with. So I am proposing a rough and ready model for the division of software engineers into only three types.

7.4 Consumer classification

But first, before presenting this model, I need to classify IT consumers. Our team relies on IT consumers for sustenance and must be structured to fit in with the consumers' environment. The matrix in Fig. 7.3 defines four basic types of consumer according to their power within the organization, and their predisposition or interest in IT.

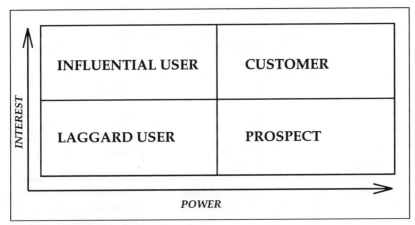

Figure 7.3 Consumer classification

Customers are people who buy systems. They have the power to decide whether or not to commission work from software teams. Their perception is business oriented — they need business solutions. Customers have choice, they decide whether you get the work or someone else does.

Prospects are potential customers. You may be able to turn them into customers by persuading them that you can identify and deliver software solutions for their business needs.

Users are people in the organization who will have to live with the systems commissioned by customers. While they have no choice, they are the people who will ultimately make the system a failure or a success. Of course, there is a full spectrum of user attitudes to IT, from the enthusiast down to the IT Luddite.

7.5 The reptilian metaphor: Toads, Chameleons and Snakes

It is as simple as that. There are three basic types of software engineer that you need to build an effective team — Toads, Chameleons and Snakes.† In the rest of this section I will summarize their characteristics so that you will be able to categorize yourself and your colleagues swiftly and accurately. More importantly I will relate these identifiable traits to the software team. This will help you to build teams that work, teams that exploit different reptile strengths to deliver useful, timely software to customers. Just to get you in the mood, here are a few key characteristics of the three reptiles:

Toads	Chameleons	Snakes
Speak technobabble	Speak technobabble and 'English'	Speak 'English'
Enjoy bugs	Do systems analysis, design and prototyping	Do business and soft systems analysis
Read manuals and science fiction	Read books	Read menus
Eat junk food	Eat plain food	Dine extravagantly
Ruggedize and tune systems	Work with users	Market to customers
Finish systems	Understand Toads and Snakes	Identify software opportunities and secure customer orders
Solve technical problems	Solve system problems	Solve business problems
Live in the IT world	Live on the interface	Live in the real world
Wear eccentric clothes	Adapt their dress to suit the environment	Wear suits

Sections 7.5.1 to 7.5.3 describe the habitats, communications skills and care and feeding of Snakes, Chameleons and Toads in more detail.

---

† OK, so snakes and chameleons are reptiles, while toads are amphibians. Somehow "cold-blooded vertebrate metaphor" just wouldn't have the same ring to it!

7.5.1 Reptile habitats

Each reptile has its own preferred ecological niche, its natural habitat; these are summarized in Fig. 7.4.

Toads live exclusively in the IT world. They even inhabit specialized niche ponds inside the IT world. There are database Toads, communications Toads, code-cutter Toads, 4GL Toads, performance and tuning Toads . . . and so on.

The Interface Zone is the strange region between IT and awkward, messy reality. Chameleons live there, together with that most dangerous species of human — people who know (or think they know) something about IT. Snakes spend most of their time in "Customer Land". They tempt people with juicy IT apples. They win the business.

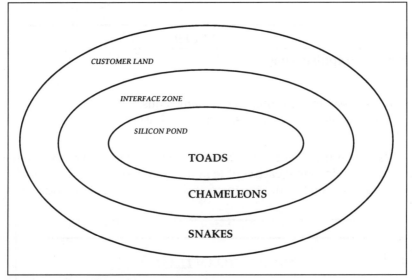

Figure 7.4 Reptile niches

7.5.2 Communication skills

In Fig. 7.5, which indicates reptile language preferences, English is really shorthand for "native language". For example, in France, this axis would be labelled French. I happen to be writing in English, so English it is.

If we consider a continuum from machine code to natural language: machine code is precise but impenetrable; natural language is rich, sometimes easy to understand, and usually rather imprecise. If we consider a class of language called technobabble, which embraces IT jargon and descends into, for example, C at the drop of a hat, we can plot the language capabilities of Toads, Chameleons and Snakes thus:

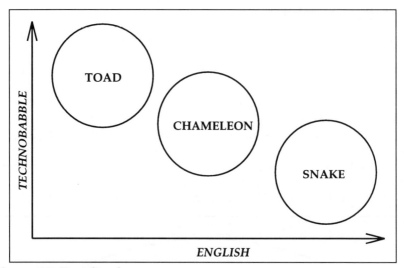

Figure 7.5 Reptilian languages

◇ Toads speak to computers and Chameleons.
◇ Chameleons speak to Toads, Snakes and users.
◇ Snakes speak to Chameleons and customers.

These communication channels are summarized in Fig. 7.6, where it should be obvious that each reptile in the team has a particular communications role, both within the team and with the outside world.

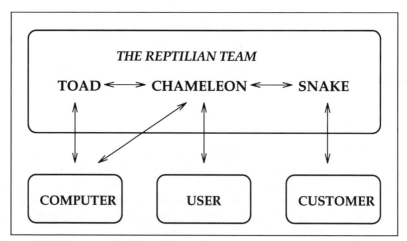

Figure 7.6 Communication channels

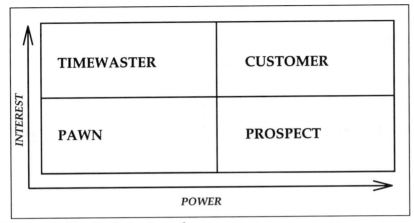

Figure 7.7 The Snake's view of consumers

7.5.3 Feeding and caring for reptiles

Each of our three reptiles has distinctly different feeding requirements. Snakes snack on customers and prospects. Their view of IT consumers is shown in Fig. 7.7.

To the Snake, customers and prospects are the only important people. These people may already be interested in what the Snake has to offer, in which case they are already customers, or they may be prospects — people that the Snake can turn into customers. Other people are of no interest to the Snake. Timewasters are more of a nuisance than pawns, because they may interfere with the customer hunt.

Snakes use sibilant sounding skills to seduce customers and prospects. They specialize in Soft Systems Analysis or Business Analysis. They use these skills to identify customer problems that they can solve and they market outline solutions to customers, securing customer ownership and commitment. Really skilled Snakes also have the capacity to recognize potential disasters and turn down work. They have a highly developed sixth sense so that they can slide away from questionable requirements.

Snakes need to be fed a steady diet of customers and prospects, otherwise they may become bored and start to bicker with the rest of the team, ultimately gobbling up Chameleons and Toads. Snakes have a continuing role throughout any software development — that of reassuring their customers, and maintaining customer commitment to the system.

The Chameleon has a different perspective on IT projects. Customers and prospects are of little interest to the Chameleon. The Chameleon needs users, preferably interested users to help to define and develop

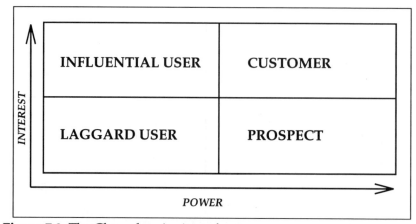

Figure 7.8 The Chameleon's view of consumers

the system. Later on, these users become even more important because they will determine the business success of the system, as shown in Fig. 7.8.

Chameleons need a constant diet of new and interesting requirements. They love the challenge of delivering 80% of a solution. Good Chameleons are skilled at systems analysis and design, and at using prototyping tools to develop most of a system. Their adaptive camouflage and language abilities means that they can swiftly fit in with different types of user and work with the user to evolve useful systems. With their independent eyes they can simultaneously identify both the users' needs, and technological options for meeting those needs.

Chameleons are opportunistic feeders. They always have both eyes open and looking for tasty users. As long as they are given a steady stream of new and interesting systems to develop they will be happy.

Chameleons are not good at finishing systems. They demand variety and are easily bored. They lack the perseverance and technical depth to "ruggedize" systems so that they are fit for release to customers. Enter the Toad (see Fig. 7.9).

Toads live on a diet of bugs (note that "the devil makes work for idle toads"). You must keep feeding them with fat, crunchy, juicy bugs. Toads are always complaining. They will croak about the part-finished systems passed on to them by Chameleons but will then get on and make the system robust, rugged and reliable. Remember the old adage "stroke a Toad and get some code".

Toads can become dangerous if they are not kept occupied with bugs. In the absence of real problems, they will invent Gothic technical solutions and compromise the systems passed to them by Chameleons.

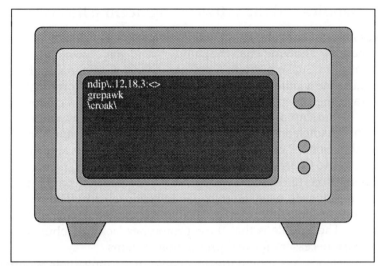

Figure 7.9 The Toad's view of the world

Toads also enjoy being rewarded with technical training courses that will allow them to become even more toady.

7.5.4 Metamorphosis and evolution

Haeckel's theory of recapitulation suggests that "each individual climbs its own evolutionary tree" [Vine and Rees, 1968]. The human embryo, for example, passes through developmental stages when it looks rather like a fish, with gills. To some extent, software engineers also recapitulate different types of reptile. Most of us go through a Toad stage, where the sheer wonder of making a machine do as we command is all that matters. Some of us move away from the Toad stage, some don't. I don't want to stretch this evolution analogy too far, because I'm not suggesting that Snakes are any further up the evolutionary chain than Toads, but, almost all IT professionals have been Toads. They may have changed into something else because they were not very good Toads.

It is a popular idea that we should strive to "develop" into something different. In general this is something to be avoided. Caterpillars may turn into butterflies, but in software engineers are best left alone. It may be possible to turn a Toad into a Chameleon or a Snake, but there is really no reason to want to. You need Toads and Chameleons and Snakes in the team to achieve success. Love and cherish them for what they are. Value their unique capabilities. Encourage them to exploit their different characteristics rather than trying to make them each more like the other.

7.5.5 Reptiles and the software engineering lifecycle

Snakes initiate the cycle. They identify prospects and develop them into customers by showing that they understand the customers' business problems. The Snake seduces customers with soft systems analysis and persuades the victim that IT can help to solve their problems. They encourage the prospect so that the prospect becomes a customer and accepts ownership of the new system. Snakes also know where to find the right Chameleons and Toads to turn the vague vision of a system into reality. Snakes get IT business, outline the solution and then hand the job over to Chameleons.

Chameleons understand enough about userspeak to be able to churn out an appropriate user interface. They work quickly. The prototypes they produce look fine, they correctly attack the customers' business priorities. The trouble is that these prototypes lack the robustness and ruggedness necessary for real production systems.

Chameleons are inherently incapable of turning their wonderful prototypes into usable systems. Perhaps it is something to do with their education and upbringing. After all, Chameleons are people who drift into computing. They are often generalists who find that IT offers an interesting but not too restrictive career. Chameleons get bored too quickly to be able to squeeze the bugs and errors out of a system. They lack the dedication and attention to detail that are needed to tune a system, or to make sure that all the components work properly.

The Toad is the real inheritor of the Dark Age programmer's mantle. Toads finish systems off. They debug the Chameleon's prototype. They tune it so that the performance is acceptable. They understand what makes the software tick. Of course, left on their own, Toads will happily fiddle with a system forever, making tiny improvements. To guard against this, the Snake must step (or slither!) in and insist that the system is delivered to the customer when it is adequate. Otherwise the Toad will tinker forever.

7.5.6 The perfect team

The perfect team has the right mix of reptiles, appropriate to the particular type of business problem that is to be tackled. If there are too many Snakes, the team will promise solutions to customers and never deliver anything. Without Snakes, the team will never get or start any useful work. Chameleons on their own are unable to identify and secure customers. They will develop half-finished prototypes for unimportant users. Without Toads, the team will never deliver working systems.

Team management is a separate issue. Any of the reptiles may turn out to have the appropriate abilities to plan, organize and control the team's work. The manager should ideally conform to Belbin's "chairman" role. The manager may come from within the team, or be some non-reptile. Once you have established the perfect team it is, of course, tempting to maintain it as a stable unit for as long as possible. Unfortunately, "possible" may not be very long at all. During the course of a project you are likely to need different Toads with different specialisms. Furthermore, Toads are such a valuable and specialized resource that they will have to hop between projects. There is a stronger case for maintaining Snake and Chameleon continuity through the life of a project. Changing Snakes will upset customers and undermine their confidence. Changing Chameleons will upset users and waste time because the incumbent Chameleon will have to learn about the user environment.

In summary, you should aim to keep a stable team of Snakes and Chameleons throughout the project, while matrix-managing Toads to get the most out of them.

7.6 I'm not a reptile — I'm an individual!

Maybe so, but I am confident that you will have no trouble in classifying your colleagues as either Snakes, Chameleons or Toads. Similarly, I am sure that they will also instantly categorize you.

About the author

John Madsen works for the Information Systems Branch, Employment Department. He used to be a Toad but has sloughed his warts and now wears a snake-skinned suit.

References and further reading

Brooks F. (1975), *The Mythical Man Month*, Addison-Wesley.

Belbin R. (1981), *Management Teams: Why they Succeed or Fail*, Heinemann.

Buchanan D. and Huczynski A. (1985), *Organizational Behaviour*, Prentice Hall.

Manpower Services Commission (1978), *Classification of Occupations and Directory of Occupational Titles*, HMSO.

Smith M. (1991), *Software Prototyping*, McGraw-Hill.

Vines A. and Rees N. (1968), *Plant and Animal Biology, Volumes I & II*, Pitman.

CHAPTER EIGHT

WOMEN IN COMPUTING
BY GILLIAN LOVEGROVE

8.1 Introduction

Women make good computer professionals. Yet the proportion of women in the profession is small and the number of women entering courses at higher educational institutions decreased in the 1980s and has stayed low. The proportion of women in senior management, in line with national trends in the public and private sector, is smaller still. There is a need to realize to the full the potential of the workforce in order to help the UK economy thrive, and women to realize their full potential. This chapter assesses the current situation, attempts to give reasons for this state of affairs and suggest strategies for improvements.

The central sections of the chapter set out the facts and issues in the areas: computing (or IT — no distinction is drawn in general) as a profession, the different perceptions of males and females, companies and the computing industry, education, equal opportunities, software analysis and design, recruitment and retention problems, the working environment and finally career progression. The conclusion sums up the present position of women in the profession and gives a prediction for the future — a prediction which is in some ways hopeful and in other ways pessimistic.

8.2 The computing profession for women: facts and figures

8.2.1 Proportions of women: higher education

In the period from the mid-1960s to 1980, the proportion of women on computing related courses was steady and of the order of 25%. Around the early 1980s the figure dropped and has remained steady at around 11% for many typical computer science courses. Hybrid degrees, especially when related to business, attract more women (of the order of 30%), whereas courses with engineering in the title, or courses residing in Engineering Faculties, attract less women (say, 6%). Research into the reasons for this phenomenon is well documented [Lovegrove and Hall, 1991; Lovegrove and Segal, 1991]. It has significance for the computing profession in that the number of women entering the profession as qualified graduates has dropped over the last ten years in proportion to the number of men, and will continue to be low.

8.2.2 Proportions of women: industry and commerce

The British Computer Society (BCS) together with Women into Information Technology (WIT) made a survey [Beech, 1990] of BCS female professional members which had two purposes:

1. To provide employers with information to enable them to attract more women into the IT profession.
2. To look at career progression and determine the factors which affect it.

The survey therefore included questions about employer type, qualifications, family size, career breaks, equal opportunities and provision of crêches and other facilities. The BCS report of 1990 showed that it has about 1800 female professional members which is about 10% of its total professional membership. Much of the information in the rest of this section is supported by the statistics given in this report.

8.2.3 Employers and working conditions

Facilities which should be offered to attract women include:

1. An equal opportunities policy which is clearly being effective.
2. Options which assist with family life and complement domestic arrangements — flexible hours, part-time working, and working at home.

3. The possibility of additional training to restore confidence as part of a career development package for women returning to work.

8.2.4 Career breaks

The majority of replies to the WIT survey indicated a career spanning ten years or more starting in the early twenties. During that time most women would have married and had children. The results confirmed that in current working conditions and social attitudes a career and family do not mix. In the survey:

1. No children, no career break — 46%.
2. Children without a career break — 24%.
3. Children with a career break — 30%.

The analysis of salary against age with and without a career break showed quite clearly that having a career break is equivalent to a reduction in salary of at least £10 000 per annum. The situation in academia varies; traditional universities may restore a person at the same salary level or even higher, whereas new universities may appoint at a lower level.

8.2.5 Recruitment and retention: why is it poor?

The recruitment in IT is fundamentally affected by attitudes in schools and in the home. Typically there is a lack of:

1. Role models at school and home.
2. Good management of computer terminals (to allow equal access to both boys and girls).
3. Good career guidance and materials.
4. Suitable software for relaxation or computer clubs.
5. Encouragement from parents for careers in computing.

This will affect recruitment in the younger age-groups, but additional reasons for low recruitment of women of all ages are:

1. The perception that computing is a career for men.
2. A computing career has a high proportion of time spent programming at the terminal.
3. A career in computing would not be fulfilling and have no human interest.
4. A career in computing requires a knowledge of computers.
5. Being good at maths is necessary to do computing.

Reasons for poor retention include:

1. Lack of self-confidence when men appear to have prior knowledge and are confident.
2. Lack of support from well-written manuals, training and supervisors.
3. There may be no "critical mass" of females around.
4. In education, much information comes from the peer group — when this is predominantly male, this is sometimes an advantage, sometimes a problem.
5. In group work, there can be an assumption that the woman will be the assistant in the subdominant, secretarial or technically undemanding role; this does not build up self-confidence and increases resentment.
6. A fear of working late at night at the office or on campus; this may include dealing with macho caretaking staff: reaching the car: using public transport. These problems unfortunately are increasing.

In some companies there is a more acute problem due to the greater tradition of the perceived need for competitive, strong, independent, "high achievement above all else" attributes.

It should be clearly asserted that some companies have addressed problems like these with good results and that not all women will find such issues arise — indeed many women enjoy working in a predominantly male environment. On the other hand, many companies do exhibit equal opportunities and many women do not enjoy sexist environments. The rest of this chapter examines why this situation exists and explores some ways to improve the situation.

8.3 Computing as a profession

8.3.1 The attributes of a good computing professional

The range of skills required by a good computing professional includes the following, starting from the more "technical" end of the spectrum and moving towards the more "communicative" skills:

⋄ The ability to solve problems; the matching of known algorithms to new problems; the development of new algorithms
⋄ Logical thinking
⋄ Abstraction; the ability to see patterns and realize possible abstractions

◇ The ability to "worry', or work, at a problem until a solution is found; persistence with problems

◇ The ability to perceive and organize the considerable quantities of detail inherent in problems, and to account for them all in implemented solutions

◇ The ability to work in a team, including non-computing users, as a contributing non-combative, non-confrontational communicating member, as a "grown-up" or "adult"

◇ The ability to communicate verbally and in writing in a clear and concise way

◇ The ability to present materials, make promotions for products, software effectively

◇ The ability to organize oneself and others within a team.

We have asserted that women make good computing professionals. Do we consider that women can make as good computing professionals as men? What do we mean by this question? Whilst many people would be astonished to think that the question might be raised, others might have a deep-rooted, though barely acknowledged prejudice, that women have less aptitude for the job. Let us consider this from two angles: one is to consider the male and female of the species "as created', or "as born" or "genetically", meaning before society or environment has had an effect. The other is to consider women and men as they are — socially and environmentally affected or conditioned.

It is generally believed that differences between the male and female as regards "technical" abilities are negligible, if they exist at all. This assertion would seem to be supported by the numbers of women in certain more popular science areas in the UK, such as biology and mathematics. It is also supported outside the UK by the large number of women in medicine in Eastern countries and by the equal numbers of women in computing professions in parts of Eastern Europe, the Middle East (at school level but not in the professions) and the Pacific Rim (China, Singapore but not Japan).

The other angle is to consider men and women conditioned by society and the UK environment. Only a minority of women enter the scientific professions, and increasingly computing is not generally regarded as a suitable occupation for women. However, this is not a reflection on women's aptitude for the computing profession and we conclude that women and men are equally capable in this respect.

This disparity in numbers between men and women means a loss of potentially valuable people from the workforce. It also has serious repercussions when we consider the attributes of those in management and senior positions. If we consider the list of abilities for the computer professional above, we see that the ones further down the list are just

those more personal or human (sometimes termed "female") characteristics that we would seek out in both men and women as team leaders or
managers. We would therefore expect to see the proportion of women in
post to rise with these levels of seniority, given the effects of society, upbringing and environment on men and women. The reverse is the case
and the effectiveness of the profession, either in commerce, industry or
academia, is reduced from its potential maximum.

8.3.2 The image of computing

Let us look at the image of computing as a subject or a profession from
various different angles, whilst indicating some of the possible implications for women.

The image of computing: UK society and the media

Imagine asking a man or woman in the street to describe a scientist,
an engineer or a computer person (interestingly there is no word for
computing professional — the nearest is computer programmer; this
fact alone is not insignificant). It is likely that the scientist would be in
a white coat and authoritative but impersonal; the engineer would be
less high ranking and holding a dirty oil-cloth. It is quite likely that the
computing person would be a man, white, strange, remote and unable
to speak intelligible English.

The engineering image in the UK has been recognized as a problem
for some time and it has been difficult to attempt to rectify the image. The
computing image is a more recent development but shows all the signs
of being as difficult to throw off. The media tend to use these stereotyped
images in all forms of entertainment, even if their science programmes
have a relatively high standard of equal opportunities representation.
Unluckily for us, the entertainment programmes have higher ratings
and influence, and perpetuate the stereotyped images.

The view of children at school

School curricula are in a state of change. On their way out are the intro-
ductions to computing through the use of raw programming techniques
like the use of Basic or Logo. Instead we are more likely to see the use of
packages. These might be through diverse parts of the curriculum, for
example: History, English, Physics or through the use of the computer
for career information held on CD-ROM.

The position of computing as a subject in schools is more likely to
be as a resource within Business than as an academic subject in its own
right. GCSEs in Computing are diminishing; GNVQs in computing skills
may replace them.

Currently, however, children see computing or IT as programming; there is less emphasis on the positive benefits that IT brings to their daily lives. This, linked with the predominance of aggressive computer games, means that the image of careers in computing is poor. Thus the discipline, as a single subject for further and higher education, attracts few girls, and arguably does not have the wider attraction for the right kind of boys either. Interestingly, there is a trend for parents to link computing with word-processing and thus do not wish either their sons or daughters to opt for such a low-rated subject.

Higher education institutions

In general courses which are hybrid (a subject "with" computing, or computing "with" a subject) attract larger numbers of girls. The purer, the more abstract, the nearer to engineering the subject appears, the less attractive it is.

Many universities, including the older establishments, offer computer science as a theoretical, more academic subject, closer to the technical, further away from the applications and business end of the subject, with software engineering and programming techniques as a key feature. Other universities, including many of the newer institutions, have widened their access by not only including this end of the spectrum but also by gearing their courses closer to industry's immediate needs rather than guardianship of the academic subject *per se*. Sometimes this includes a greater stress on systems analysis and design, group working, use of CASE tools and presentation skills. Other universities offer information systems as a degree course where knowledge of programming is required as a basic skill but not over-emphasized, with a greater weight given to the user's needs and extraction of information and knowledge together with skills of communication, organization and documentation.

Unfortunately an orientation towards the "hard", more technical areas of computer science and software engineering, coupled with a downgrading of the "soft" human issues, is pervasive in British universities, and is often reflected in the funding and general support for information systems courses and research. Information systems research sits uncomfortably between science, social science and business funding bodies, though the Government and Europe have made some attempts to fund through cross-discipline projects. In summary, the very aspects of computing that appeal most to women are those that are least recognized and least supported in education.

Greater numbers of women are entering the hybrid courses and a greater proportion of these are in the former polytechnics. No statistics are available for the intellectual ability of these undergraduates. Whether the more able women computing-oriented undergraduates are thus going to former polytechnics as opposed to established universities, or whether the more able women are studying more traditional single subjects, and not computing, is a matter for speculation. It seems a reasonable proposition that a significant number of women come into this latter category: a sufficient loss by any reckoning not to be ignored.

The image of computing: other older professionals

Well-educated professionals from other disciplines aged over forty probably did very little or no computing as part of their early education and by and large are unaware of the current professional standards required, including the proper training. They are not aware that computing is now as professional a career as their own. It is a commonly recognized difficulty within the computing community that anyone with some experience using computer packages, or having taught themselves a programming language, believes that this skill is all that is required. This is exacerbated by the rapidly changing nature of computing technology.

These well-educated people are in influential positions in companies, industry, government departments and research councils; yet they have this poorly informed view of computing. They may well be the parents of potential undergraduates in computing. They may not see computing as a professional career by and large; arguably they would see it as acceptable through pressure for their sons but potentially unfulfilling for their daughters. The influence of peer group and parents on boys and girls is, of course, great.

8.4 Male/Female perceptions

Men and women are different. *Vive la différence!* It enriches our lives. However, it gives rise to unanticipated problems of values and even language [Spender, 1990; Tannen, 1992].

8.4.1 Lack of knowledge of the problem

There is generally a lack of awareness and knowledge concerning male and female perceptions of each other, the differences in these perceptions, and consequently the resulting effects of these different perceptions. The feminist movement and women's studies have increased the interest and focus, and quite possibly the prejudice, in this direction. It is not surprising therefore that the subject areas which are traditionally a male stronghold are also the areas which have the least awareness and appreciation of the problems. This is largely because men in those areas have not had cause to think issues through and to appreciate the problems. Changes in behaviour and attitudes take time to come about, and the progressive equal opportunities thinking in science, technology, engineering and computing is only beginning.

The software product

With regards to computing, in particular, it should be self-evident that software should be designed for the real users, and thus systems analysts need to be fully aware and sensitive to the needs of the user. We would assert that women, with their greater awareness of the needs of others, and greater powers of orthogonal thinking, will in general be better systems analysts. (Once again we recognize that some men have these abilities too and we are making assertions in general terms.)

There is evidence that software has been of poor quality because not enough attention has been given to the requirements capture and analysis; the user's needs have not been met. The BCS Code of Conduct, for example, makes no reference to gender. Yet the needs of a female user might be significantly different from those of a male; these might have been overlooked even when female users will be in the majority. We would assert that this is the case in a not insignificant number of instances and some of them are recent [Green et al., 1993].

Take, for example, the design of the point-of-sale in Sainsbury's, which is an engineering example, but will serve as an illustration. Any woman less than six foot tall will tell you that it is uncomfortable or impossible to sign a cheque on the high ledge provided (a height designed for tall men presumably), that the ledge wobbles sufficiently to distort a signature, and that the cheque has instead to be signed wedged amongst the shopping. How much were needs of the users of the system taken into account?

Of course, it would be easy for male systems analysts to rectify the above problem, but would they just be dealing with the symptoms and not the underlying malady?

8.4.2 Upbringing

Women are from an early age by and large encouraged to conform, to be pleasing to both men and women, not to be controversial, to be clean and tidy, to work conscientiously, to be unselfish and to work for the greater good. In short, they like to do good and be good. Thus when once in post alongside men, they are likely to be good workers, to contribute by taking on the organizational tasks, to have better than average attendance records, to work extra hours at home. On the downside; from an early age, women are generally discouraged from voicing controversial opinions.

This attitude can affect the amount of self-esteem of the young woman. Even women who are very self-confident may well feel the pressure to conform which may later make them less likely to fulfil their true potential and rise to the position of which they are capable [Dowling, 1982].

Another example of conformance affecting the way people behave might be in the context of men and women looking at a job description with say ten requirements. A woman might see four she does not satisfy and will not consider applying, whereas a man might see five that he does satisfy and, ignoring the rest, will apply for the job.

8.4.3 People relating to people

People need to relate to other people to feel comfortable that they are acceptable. In greeting, light conversation might include the weather, for example, and other topics may be comfortable to both genders. Men will relate to each other in ways which are often foreign to women, for example, talking about the latest football results. In the context of a wide variety of common exchanges, these occurrences are unimportant but if these are the only ways of greeting at the beginnings of meetings, women will feel as estranged as a man might feel in a group of women chatting about a largely feminine topic. The effect on the woman in the man's group in making her feel isolated might be to make her more assertive about making points in a discussion, in order to make her presence felt; this is not uncommon and can lead to the woman being regarded as out of line. For a man isolated amongst women, he too feels the greater need to be assertive and to dominate, which is equally unacceptable to the women.

Problems and progress within computing

Some women (and some men if they admit it) find it difficult to overcome the feelings of inferiority when faced with common male behaviour in a learning environment; namely, showing off or bravado. Manuals for new systems may not be sufficiently user-friendly. Women, with their conditioning not to make a fuss and to conform, may find it more difficult to ask direct questions.

Working in teams is common but sometimes there is little knowledge of group dynamics and their significance. There may be little appreciation of the needs of the females or lone female of the team and the support which she may require.

The appraisal can form the basis for open discussion of problems and presents opportunities to redress the balance. Also, many companies are attempting mentoring schemes with varying degrees of success.

Where it works well, the advantages are in the support of the person being mentored, seeing at first hand or hearing about the ways in which situations are handled and the mentor acting as a role model with hard practical advice.

Environment and working environment

We have observed that men and women have different perceptions; the consequences are serious and not to be underestimated. They arise through a lack of understanding of the opposite sex and are based on entrenched attitudes. For example, women in the male-dominated computing profession must cope with the following:

◇ The after-work drink in the bar: statistics would show that women do not participate as frequently as men. The reasons may be various, but the fact remains that they are missing when tactics and ideas are being discussed. Yet everyone knows that face-to-face meetings break down communication difficulties and tend to bond people together, especially whilst having an alcoholic drink.
◇ Men relate to each other by means of exchanging information on football, cars or such. They may well relate to each other by making remarks about women or sex, with no intention of offence. There is an onus on women to understand this and deal with it in any way they find suitable but for many it leaves them feeling uncomfortable rather than affiliated. Most men do not understand why.

8.4.4 Male measures for women

It takes time for men to realize that the criteria they have used on their peer group for evaluation of each other may not simply be extended to women; by using these criteria, they are being unjust. Examples of mistaken measures are:

◇ People tend to appoint people like themselves.
◇ Paper qualifications (as a reflection of capability, they weight favourably towards men).
◇ Quieter, less assertive attitudes (men are more likely to seize attention in meetings; women tend to wait to be asked).

This has resulted in women needing to be more than good enough in terms of qualifications, when being measured against men. Also women may undervalue themselves as they unconsciously pick up the surrounding men's opinions of themselves rather than being able to make objective judgements for themselves. Another effect may be that male managers may not be prepared to put women to the same testing experiences as men, or place responsibilities their way, thus depriving them of the opportunity to shine or learn from mistakes. Sometimes this happens through a wish to protect the woman.

This has particular weight in respect of career progression and is developed further in Section 8.6.

8.5 Equal Opportunities

8.5.1 Legislation

The Equal Pay Act 1970 and the Sex Discrimination Acts of 1975 and 1986 have direct effect on employment decisions in relation to equality of opportunity for men and women. The Sex Discrimination Act 1975 established the Equal Opportunities Commission (EOC) which has the following duties:

1. To eliminate sex and marriage discrimination.
2. To promote equal opportunities between the sexes.
3. To monitor both the Sex Discrimination Act and the Equal Pay Act.

The Equal Opportunities Commission has published a wide variety of booklets including *Guidelines for Equal Opportunities Employers* [EOC, 1986], whilst Straw sets the equal opportunities movement in its legislative framework and places equal opportunity in employment at the heart of good personnel and business practice [Straw, 1989].

8.5.2 The Equal Pay Act 1970 (as amended 1983)

An employee is entitled to equal pay (and other contractual terms and conditions) with an employee of the opposite sex if:

1. They are doing work which is the same or broadly similar.
2. They are doing work which has been rated as equivalent by an analytical job evaluation scheme.
3. They are doing work of an equal value in terms of the demands made on the worker (whether or not there has been a job evaluation scheme).

8.5.3 The Sex Discrimination Acts 1975 and 1986

Direct sex discrimination occurs when one person is treated less favourably, on the ground of their sex, than a person of the other sex is or would be treated in similar circumstances.

Indirect sex discrimination occurs when a requirement or condition, which cannot be justified on grounds other than sex, is applied to men and women equally but has the effect, in practice, of disadvantaging a considerably higher proportion of one sex than the other. For example, if you demand technical qualifications which few women possess, and which are not necessary for the job, this would constitute indirect sex discrimination against a woman without those qualifications.

There is confusion between positive discrimination and positive action. "Positive discrimination" describes the situation where appointments are made on grounds other than those which are job-related. Discrimination on grounds of race or gender (except where a genuine occupational qualification exists) at the point of selection is unlawful in the UK.

There can be positive action by employers under these Acts. "Positive action" does not occur at the point of selection. Its starting point is a recognition that each individual has different needs. Discrimination in society has deprived minority ethnic groups and women of opportunities which may in turn mean that they will not have acquired the experience considered necessary to perform a particular job. A positive provision is that any person may lawfully provide training for employment for people — even if they happen to be mainly women — who are in special need of training because they have spent a period away from full-time work through discharging domestic responsibilities. In addition, an employer may encourage members of that sex only, to take up that work — for example, by advertisements which encourage applications from women. However, when the time comes actually to select people for these jobs, there must be no discrimination — applicants must be treated on merit regardless of sex.

8.5.4 Sexual harassment

Sexual harassment as such is not specifically outlawed by the Sex Discrimination Act 1975, but the Court of Session established in *Strathclyde Council v. Porcelli* (1986) that it can amount to direct sex discrimination: a person discriminates against a woman if "on the grounds of her sex he treats her less favourably than he treats or would treat a man". Racial and sexual harassment are difficult to define in terms of what is acceptable behaviour. Sexual harassment means unwanted conduct of a sexual nature, or other conduct based on sex, affecting the dignity of women and men at work. This can include unwelcome physical, verbal or non-verbal conduct.

In the Council of Europe Declaration, 92/C27/01, the European Commission recommends that member states encourage employers and employee representatives to develop measures to implement the Commission's Code of Practice on the protection of women and men at work. This Code of Practice:

1. Draws the distinction between consensual behaviour, which is never regarded as sexual harassment and conduct which is not desired by the recipient.
2. Makes clear that what is offensive is essentially subjective in that it is for the recipient to determine.
3. Illustrates that sexual harassment covers not only sexual overtures but also sex-based abuse of power.
4. Links the offensive conduct to its effect on the employee's working environment.

There are some misconceptions with respect to sexual harassment. For example, some people believe that it is only natural for men to make a pass at women. It is because of the male and female roles ascribed to and learned by men and women in our society that there is confusion as to what is natural male behaviour and what is learned behaviour. Sexual harassment is learned social behaviour.

There are many different behaviours which constitute sexual harassment. As it is the recipient of the behaviour who decides whether or not they feel sexually harassed, it is important to give them the autonomy to decide. Behaviour or actions which constitute sexual harassment may take many forms and can include requests for sexual favours, leers, physical contact, sexist remarks, dirty jokes, pin-ups, explicit sexual comments, innuendo and remarks about a person's body. Verbal sexual harassment, for example, is a form of harassment frequently ignored by people in positions of power. Unfortunately the recipients of sexual harassment are often not in a position to say "no" or for their words and actions to be respected. Sexual harassment is not a rare phenomenon. What is still unusual is for sexual harassment to be properly labelled and to be taken seriously.

8.5.5 Opportunity 2000

Opportunity 2000 is a "Business in the Community" initiative to improve the balance of men and women in the workforce. It is founded on the business case that women are an underused resource in terms of investment in training and development, and that there is a resulting lost potential. It is a non-politically aligned initiative with some two hundred and sixteen organizations as members, from both the private and public sector. It facilitates the sharing of good practice through networking, seminars, advice and publications.

Key organizations have committed themselves to attaining specific goals. They have taken a critical look at their internal operations and established a realistic, tailored and practical Action Plan. Through peer pressure Opportunity 2000 will influence other employers to develop their own equal opportunity programmes.

8.5.6 Equal opportunities employers

The EOC recommends that the easiest way of becoming an equal opportunities employer is first to formulate a written equal opportunities policy and objectives. Littlewoods, for example, have a positive action programme to support their EO policy:

1. An EO Policy Statement is displayed on all notice boards.
2. Statistical reports on the position of women, black people, ethnic minority groups and disabled people within Littlewoods are monitored quarterly.
3. Changes are made to recruitment, training and career development practices as necessary.
4. Realistic goals are set, with yearly targets, to achieve their long-term objectives for employment of women, black people, members of ethnic minority groups and disabled people.
5. EO performance is included in the yearly appraisal scheme for managers.

8.6 Career progression issues

There are few who would contend the proposition that the more women in senior posts in computing, the better — for reasons such as being a role model for staff and for recruitment, for their management skills and possibly above all, for a refreshing and stimulating view based on their different life experience.

What do we see as good role models for younger women? The few women professors and senior managers that exist are likely to have no children or be divorced and will be very focused on their own achievements (the exceptions being those appointed under more enlightened criteria). Meanwhile due to their greater numbers, the men in high positions provide role models across a spread of abilities; some good, some narrowly focused.

8.6.1 Attitude of promotion deciders

Men often have a high regard for achievement; for example, setting themselves goals and reaching them visibly before their peer group. From a promotion point of view, women are often hampered in that they have less regard for achievement for its own sake and have a greater regard for doing a job well.

Older professors or managers may recognize young aspiring men as similar to themselves at that age and favour them as potential high-flyers over women; similarly, they may write off older women who are perhaps re-establishing themselves for another career burst as not being worth investing in, or encouraging. They are unaware and fail to recognize the established fact that women over forty, once freed of child care, have the potential to progress at a marked faster rate than before.

8.6.2 Qualifications

Here are some of the reasons why many (but not all) women are at a disadvantage:

1. If they have taken a career break, they will not be as up to date in the latest technology and methods of working.
2. If they have taken a career break, they will have lost their position inside the group with respect to their contemporaries and in academia may find themselves isolated.
3. They are unlikely to be able to work outside the 9-to-5 office hours for reasons of children, even though they can work late at home.
4. Women are often better communicators and organizers and will be encouraged to take more of the administration jobs than their share; time given to administration cannot be given to technical development or research, so they are undermining their own case for promotion.

8.6.3 Aptitude

Apart from qualifications for the job in the absolute, what about aptitude for the job? How do we measure aptitude? We use our experience from the past in trying to recognize abilities. If men are judging men and women in assessing aptitude, how much more difficult is it for them to recognize aspiring women? For example, to become a professor of computing, it is necessary to establish a highly creditable research record, even though the main function of this professor is likely to include the management of a group of lecturers and a sound knowledge of business and finance as well as research.

Much of the above applies to academic and industrial career progression but in academia there are in addition some important differences. The first observation to make is that by and large there is less overt prejudice against women than in industry, but more is hidden. The second observation is deadly; criteria for career progression in academia are deep-rooted in traditions centuries old which neither take into account a fast changing subject like computing nor are they equally fair to men and women.

8.6.4 Career progression into management

Efforts to recruit women into the computing professions are continuing, but what about progression from initial posts into middle and senior management? The figures would seem to indicate that computing career progression is very much in line with other careers and that although the figures are poor, there is by and large no better or worse career progression. The problem lies with the well-known "glass ceiling" which is a barrier invisible from above and prevents women's progress into more responsible and senior positions. The EOC maintains that only 4% of important middle management posts are held by women and fewer than 2% of senior executive posts. The UK lags behind the USA where there are affirmative action programmes for women [King, 1993].

Much management training and theory now are in fact the feminine way of doing things. Whereas traditional practice was strong, authoritarian and combative, modern management training advocates communication and leading by example [McLoughlin, 1992]. Women can be especially good at building efficient and effective teams; they will seek to ensure cooperation rather than competition within the workplace.

Computing technology is changing rapidly, causing pressures on all people in the profession, including management. To make the greatest use of the able women and men available makes sense. Yet the statistics show that it is harder for a woman to progress in her career compared with a man. The computing profession is being wasteful of its talent.

8.7 Strategies

8.7.1 National initiatives

Women into Information Technology (WIT)

WIT was launched in 1988 and concentrates on the IT sector of industry. The Council of Directors for WIT is made up of representatives from major technical UK firms and professional organizations. It is thus an employer-led campaign whose objective is to broaden the main human resources priorities and policies of IT employers as well as educators and trainers.

Initially there was Department of Trade and Industry funding to start up the campaign and to encourage employer participation in funding. This ceased after a few years at the same point as the recession was in progress. Recently the WIT Foundation has concentrated more on becoming an information source and an enabling force and as such provides a valuable role.

Women into Science and Engineering (WISE)

WISE was launched in 1984 by the Equal Opportunities Commission and the Engineering Council and its aim was to encourage women to take up careers in science and engineering and to encourage industry to consider positively the employment of women, particularly at higher professional and technical levels of employment.

With a longer establishment and the backing of the Engineering Council, WISE is probably the best known of the national campaigns. Most schools have had a visit from the WISE bus and children are familiar with the aim of encouraging women into science and engineering. WISE does encourage girls into computing as part of the campaign but clearly placed amongst the other careers in science and engineering.

Women into Computing (WiC)

The Women into Computing movement originated in 1988 following a conference at Lancaster which revealed the national phenomenon of a fall in the percentage of girls entering computing courses at universities and sought to establish the reasons for this. With its roots in academia, the organization now exists to coordinate and promote activities mainly in the educational sector designed to make women aware of the opportunities for worthwhile and fulfilling careers in computing.

The movement's major achievement is a bi-annual conference at which there are active workshops and it provides a forum for discussion of problems. Its role has become mainly that of a support group for women in computing in academia.

Strategies for national campaigns

Any effort which causes a spotlight to be placed on women in their occupations is bound to be helpful, as raising awareness amongst men of the issues for women, and having more than a superficial acceptance of ideas is most important. The more money that goes into these campaigns, the more successful they will be. Whether led by employers or by government, without money they are limited in success.

Employers need to survive and in recession they have to focus on survival. They often plan for the coming year rather than the next five. Thus as far as women are concerned they are likely to consider employing skilled returners but are unwilling to invest in projects for younger age groups where the payback is less immediate.

It requires a government policy, with a longer-term view, including education, to be effective. The need for a more highly skilled workforce has been asserted by Government, yet the encouragement of women into higher education in science engineering and computing is low on their priority list. Is this because they do not see the efficacy of such a policy? Why do they not provide a much more effective publicity campaign for careers in computing in schools, with appropriate materials?

8.7.2 The British Computer Society and other bodies

The British Computer Society (BCS) states that it is committed to equal opportunities and to Opportunity 2000, and has backed the WIT Foundation, so helping to produce the Beech report [Beech, 1990]. However, the proportion of women in its own hierarchy is low particularly at the higher levels; strategic committee meetings are held with no women present. This is symptomatic of the lack of positive action in favour of women for which the Opportunity 2000 campaign is striving.

Similarly, whilst broadcasting the value of equal opportunities in the profession, the BCS has a Code of Conduct that — until the current version was written — used "he" throughout, which makes it appear to have been written by men for men. Language *does* matter.

Apart from rewording its own Code of Conduct there are other ways in which the BCS, itself, can more actively support equal opportunities for women at minimal cost. These include:

1. Positive discrimination and active encouragement of women to apply for Council membership.
2. Funding, or seeking funding through industrial links, for a schools' video on careers in computing, in an equal opportunity manner.
3. Producing a code of conduct to promote equal opportunities at all levels, including senior management and mummy-track staff development (a faster track for women who have recently had children, or recently relinquished a major caring role within the family).
4. More actively supporting the production of software of quality which takes into account the needs of women and men.
5. Monitoring equal opportunity practices more rigorously than at present, with a more positive code of conduct.
6. More effective marketing of computing as a profession of value, thus raising its profile amongst the other professions.

Similar support can be given by the Institution of Electrical Engineers and the Engineering Council which have greater funds and apparently greater appreciation of the problems of gender inequality in the profession. Similarly, the Higher Education Fundings Council for England (HEFCE) could be effective in requiring education departments to show how they are meeting their equal opportunities objectives.

8.7.3 Companies and universities

There is a wide variation in the adoption of the ideas of Opportunity 2000 in companies. Some, such as IBM, are attempting to attain similar standards to their American counterparts. Others are in need of a deeper change in culture to make equal opportunity measures effective. For example, the UK has one of the worst reputations in Europe for nursery provision, though improvements in some companies are being made.

Perceptions

Staff development is important in any company or institution. For example, training for new computing methods is a necessity. Similarly, time can be set aside to consider equal opportunities for women, including an awareness of the different perceptions of men and women and male values and so on. Most decision makers believe they are fulfilling equal opportunity requirements by giving women equal consideration (under male values) with men for promotion or recruitment. With better training they would realize this is not sufficient. Behaving in a more enlightened manner would lead over a number of years to a change in attitude.

Strategies for staff recruitment

Rather than relying upon paper qualifications, a greater acknowledgement of the expectations of women and the contribution of their experience of life would increase the number of women on the staff. With few exceptions, women provide at the minimum a solid, conscientious contribution to a group, frequently working longer hours and fitting better into the group structure, even if their paper qualifications are lower. This might be said to be asking for positive discrimination, but actually is looking at aptitude for the job rather than paper qualifications.

Career progression

The common cry is, "We would love to appoint women if only they were as equally qualified as men". We would assert that there are more women who would be equally capable in the jobs to which they are attempting to be promoted; it is in the perceptions and values of the male-dominated panel members who make the decisions that the problems lie. The old adage that a woman has to prove herself several times over compared with a man is not without foundation.

Why do promotion panels need encouragement to positive action as regards appointing women? Clearly it is because they feel the risks are greater. Yet the statistics indicate no greater risk. And so less women reach higher positions; and those that do, have had to sacrifice spare time and families to focus and achieve over and above that required of a man. Clearly, with positive action, there could be some poor appointments, but on average the women would be at least as equal as their peers.

The university curriculum and its assessment

It is important to try to improve the proportion of women on university courses from its current low value in order to increase the number of well-qualified women in the computing profession.

Titles of degrees and the position in the School or Faculty structure are important. The proportions of women on the same computing award in a School of Engineering, a School of Computing or a School of Business would be significantly different. Putting "Engineering" into an award title is a deterrent for women, even if it has the word "Software" in front of it. To give the same award a title including the word "Business" increases its attraction, quite possibly for men also. The recent trend to ally awards with engineering to increase status with respect to the Engineering Council or HEFCE has backfired with respect to proportions of women.

It is worthwhile considering how to improve the attractiveness of computing course content whilst maintaining the quality of subject material. One possibility is to include more of the human aspects subjects, either as core or options. These might include a greater proportion of information systems curricula, psychology and sociology, and might contain lesser proportions of subjects like logic circuits, assembler and configuration management. Variations might be to include business and management. Such courses may well be as attractive to men as well as women: men who might otherwise not enter the computing profession, and the profession needs such men and women.

Another objective of awards is to educate for employment. There will be an increasing trend for graduates to find employment designing multimedia and information systems for the workplace, requiring not only a specialist knowledge of computing but also the skill of assessing tasks and organizational structures. This softer end of information systems should be included in more curricula.

There is in most computing courses some assessment by group work; this needs to be carefully managed to provide equal opportunities, avoiding male dominance and female subdominance (e.g. taking up the secretary role).

There also has to be careful management of final year project selection to provide equal opportunities. It has been shown that capable female students are often underestimated by male teachers because they are not showing typical capable-male characteristics (they tend to be quieter, show off less, and may ask questions looking for support more frequently) despite good assessment results. Without due care and attention, the best projects may be allocated to men and opportunities for the women to excel are diminished.

8.7.4 UK society and the media

The media can help by maintaining their current position on equal opportunities in science, technology, engineering and computing programmes. They could also help raise awareness of the problems of the male/female perceptions described earlier in this chapter.

Making serious inroads into UK society's approach to girls' and boys' upbringing and the resulting sex-stereotyping is a very difficult task. Indeed the only way to achieve this quickly would probably be via mass coverage in the media. However, in the UK we are comfortable reinforcing our own sexual identities by reinforcing the male/female identities in our children and it is extremely unlikely that the media would see a need for change in this direction; their popularity ratings would drop. Realistically, the change is likely to occur more slowly due to pressure from the women in our society having greater influence in the home and by having more spending powers.

8.8 Concluding remarks

There is a recognized need for a highly trained and skilled workforce to help the UK economy thrive and that the training of this workforce will take some years of investment. There is a greater loss to the economy of the UK due to not realizing to the full the potential of the workforce; one way to help achieve this aim is to encourage more women into these professions and more women into senior management.

Apart from the economy of the UK, what are the implications of few women at management levels? Tomorrow's world will contain a greater amount of teaching and learning; probably via multimedia, email systems and computing in the home, available to all. If women are not around to advise on the design of these systems, including the content of the software, then it is unlikely that full equal opportunities can be achieved; computing will be continue to be seen as a male-dominated subject.

There has been an obvious change in the media in recent years. Advertisements have changed radically towards women, often at the expense of men, because of the increasing power of female buying power. Can we hope for a similar change in professional attitudes in computing and engineering? Can we hope for equal numbers of men and women in computing? Unfortunately not to same extent, as the economic need is not sufficiently clear, and effective strategies to change attitudes are not clear. Progress towards equal numbers of men and women in the computing workforce is likely to be slow but gradual, due to the greater widespread use of educational computing tools and slowly increasing numbers of women using technology in their professions. The outlook is even more bleak at the more technical engineering end of the computing spectrum, as it is unlikely that society will accept engineering as a suitable occupation for women.

Much of the academic research into women in computing arose out of the observations in the 1980s of the drop in percentage of women entering degree courses in computing. There has been a belief and a hope that this might be rectified in the short term. On the contrary, it seems that this phenomenon is here to stay and unless degree courses radically alter their curriculum to be attractive to girls, and unless there is a greater knowledge of the range of careers, fully up to date, in computing in schools, only 11% or so of graduates in computing will be female.

Women will, however, continue to join the computing profession at a more mature age, probably from other professions or as returners to work. So the overall percentage of women in computing will be maintained at 10–15%, instead of the 50% it could be. These women who join later in life need an accelerated career track and then the proportion of women at senior management in computing might move above 2%.

There is much that needs to be done to ensure that society does not lose out.

Acknowledgments

I wish to acknowledge the help of Judy Emms and Jennifer Stapleton in the production of this chapter. Judy contributed many ideas to its themes and Jennifer gave insights into the industrial setting, which were invaluable. Also I would like to thank Maureen Atkinson, Alan Eardley, Geoff Crum, Christine King, Chris Mann, Colin Myers, Ellen Neighbour Pat Pearce and Chris Whitehouse for reading the drafts and contributing ideas.

About the author

Dr Gillian Lovegrove is Head of Information Systems at Staffordshire University, where she is research leader of the object-oriented technology research group and directs the Staffordshire IT EQUATE project, which promotes equal opportunities for girls in computing.

She recognizes the importance of her appearance, believes that variety is the spice of life, often dresses up for the occasion but rebels from time to time. Her favourite suit is classic, expensive and enjoyable to wear.

References and further reading

Beech C. (1990), *Women and WIT: A Survey of the Female Professional Members of the BCS*, British Computer Society.

Dana D. (1990), *Talk it out*, Kogan Page.

Davidson M. and Cooper C. (eds) (1992), *Shattering the Glass Ceiling*, Paul Chapman Publishing.

Dowling C. (1982), *The Cinderella Complex*, Fontana.

Dowling C. (1988), *Perfect Women*, Fontana.

EOC (1986), *Guidelines for Equal Opportunities Employers*.

Firth-Cozens J. and West M. (eds) (1991), *Women at Work*, Open University Press.

Friday N. (1977), *My Mother, My Self*, Fontana.

Green E., Owen J. and Pain D. (1993), *Gendered by Design*, Taylor and Francis.

King C. (1993), *Through The Glass Ceiling*, Tudor Business Publishing.

Lovegrove G. and Hall W. (1991), *Where are all the girls now?* in [Lovegrove and Segal, 1991] pp 33–44.

Lovegrove G. and Segal B. (eds) (1991), *Women into Computing: Selected Papers 1988–1990*, Springer-Verlag.

McLoughlin J. (1992), *Up and Running, Women in Business*, Virago.

Richardson D. and Robinson V. (1993), *Introducing Women's Studies*, Macmillan.

Roddick A. (1991), *Body and Soul*, Ebury Press.

Savage M. and Witz A. (eds) (1992), *Gender and Bureaucracy*, Blackwells.

Shapiro J. (1993), *Men: A Translation for Women*, Avon.

Spender D. (1990), *Man Made Language*, Pandora.

Steinem G. (1992), *Revolution from Within: A Book of Self-Esteem*, Corgi.

Straw J. (1989), *Equal Opportunities*, Institute of Personnel Management.

Tannen D. (1992), *You Just Don't Understand: Women and Men in Conversation*, Virago.

CHAPTER NINE

CONFESSIONS OF A SOFTWARE QUALITY ADDICT

BY TRACY HALL

9.1 Introduction

Almost weekly we hear about the atrocious quality of our software systems — £10 million wasted on a useless computer system at Wessex Health Authority, the failure of London's ambulance system, DSS computers paying out more money than they should have done, and so on. In such a climate it is not surprising that software quality is currently fashionable. Yet another "silver bullet". However, the industry has already had many supposed silver bullets — CASE, Formal Methods, Object Oriented Design and SSADM, to name only a few. The problem is that the previous silver bullets are either technical computer-based systems and tools or else more sophisticated software development methodologies — as you might expect, people within the software industry are basically technophiles. They are as keen to develop computer-based systems and tools to solve their own problems as they are to develop them for any other industry, so computer-based solutions to the quality crisis are profligate.

However, so far none of these computer-based quality innovations have actually lived up to their initial claims. Indeed, the evidence now suggests that the software produced using, for example, CASE is actually of poorer quality. This serves to illustrate another problem, in that new tools and methods have frequently been introduced into software development more in a vain hope that they will improve software quality than on the basis of any hard evidence. Fortunately, people are now starting to realize that we might actually improve software quality by more systematic and objective management of the technology that we already have, rather than by introducing even more technology. This is where Software Quality Management (SQM) comes into play.

SQM takes a step back from the technologies that now make up a modern software development environment, and instead looks at how all these technologies are actually being used and managed. After all, there is no point in relying on technological innovation to solve the current software quality problems as any technical innovation will probably be obsolete in five years' time. Today's software development environments are so complex that it is only by concentrating on improving the working practices used within these environments that software quality can be improved in the long run. SQM provides a framework with which to introduce and manage new technologies in a controlled, rather than haphazard, way.

It is becoming increasingly clear that the management of software development has not kept pace with technological advancement. Software management is the weak link where software quality is concerned. This proposition is lucidly evidenced by a study undertaken by Capers Jones [Jones, 1994]. This study suggests that whilst technical staff are, on the whole, performing well, their management are performing consistently less well.

Quality Management Systems have been successfully used for many years by other industries. A prime example is the manufacturing industry. They have also been used for many years by the Japanese software industry. So contrary to the belief of many people in the Western World's software industry, it is not a new idea to produce something within a quality management framework. Introducing quality-oriented working practices into software development is really nothing more than taking advantage of the things that others have already learnt. However, it is probably only now, as software engineering matures from a craft to an engineering discipline, that the industry is in a position to adopt some really rather standard practices — whilst at the same time thinking it is being revolutionary!

In today's competitive climate no industry or individual organization, whether in the public or private sector, can afford not to produce quality products. Some say that this was the main reason for the failure of the Communist world. Similarly, the main reason for Japan's success is its ability to consistently produce quality goods. Clearly, if quality can have such a profound impact on whole countries then it can also have a similar impact on individual organizations.

The current notion of software quality does, however, remain a maligned one. Many people still seem to think (or hope!) that "quality" is just the latest fad. Unfortunately, the following comment is still as true now as it ever was:

> The problem with quality management is not what people know about it. The problem is what they think they know about it [Crosby, 1979].

In response to such an unfortunate situation, this chapter tries to answer some of the typical questions that people in the software industry ask about quality. Most of the questions asked are valid, but some of them suggest that many software professionals are rather shell-shocked. This state is probably the result of two things. First, bitter past experiences of all the other miracle cures. Second, developers know that the management in software engineering is generally poor and that introducing quality management is not going to help. This second point is very important. Whilst setting up quality working practices should be effective at improving software quality, if it is introduced and managed badly, then people will be right to be sceptical. No SQM is going to make up for an underlying deficit in management ability. A basic level of sound management is a prerequisite to the introduction of any quality mechanisms.

The rest of this chapter is divided into the following broad sections. Section 9.2 addresses general quality definition issues, Section 9.3 answers questions which focus on specific software quality mechanisms and Section 9.4 contains questions which relate to the perceived and actual problems of introducing software quality mechanisms.

9.2 Defining quality

9.2.1 Introduction

The term "quality" is applicable to any product or service; hence much of any discussion about quality is just as applicable to a cup of tea as it is to nuclear reactor software. This section looks at both the generalities of quality and the specifics of software quality. It also introduces the concept of formal quality certification.

9.2.2 What is quality?

Everyone, in all walks of life, has a vested interest in obtaining good-quality products and services. Unfortunately, it is impossible to define quality. Quality means different things to different people and is different within different contexts. However, people usually have no difficulty at all recognizing a good-quality product or service when they see one. This dilemma is summed up nicely by Barbara Kitchenham of the National Computer Centre:

> hard to define, impossible to measure, easy to recognize [Kitchenham, 1989]

Many people think something that is of good quality must be the best, the most expensive and exclusive. Indeed the *Oxford English Dictionary* (OED) supports this view of quality by defining it as:

Degree of excellence, unconstrained by cost [OED, 1990].

This is an unhelpfully narrow view of quality. Most people do not obtain the absolute best product or service but can rightly regard what they do obtain as good quality. Furthermore, the OED view of quality presupposes that there is actually an absolute level of quality to aspire to, which is not usually the case. Let's look at an example. Say you had to travel from London to Newcastle. Clearly there are lots of means by which you could complete the journey (car, plane, bus, helicopter, train, bicycle, foot and so on). Each of these could provide a good-quality journey. In deciding which mode of transport to use you would use many different factors to assess the likely quality of the journey. The kind of quality factors that you would be interested in could include:

◇ Cost
◇ Time
◇ Reliability
◇ Comfort
◇ Environmental impact
◇ Safety

In this case, for example, the comfort factor may well be in competition with a desire for a highly "green" journey, in which case one quality factor will have to be compromised in favour of another. Similarly, cost or safety factors may constrain all the other factors.

Quality is multi-dimensional. It is made up of many, often competing, factors. Each factor may be weighted differently in different circumstances and differently by different people. In our example, a student will almost certainly weight the journey factors differently from a business person. Even then, the student will probably think differently if, for example, they were on their way to see their mother in intensive care.

In this example travelling to Newcastle by train may be a good-quality solution to some people whilst not to others.

Quality is not an absolute attribute of any entity, so defining quality for all situations and all products in not appropriate. Equally, whilst people often "instinctively" know what quality they are looking for, it is hard to pin down what constitutes the quality of an entity — whatever that entity is.

9.2.3 What is software quality?

Characterizing software quality is complex because of the complex nature of a software product. Here are some of the many software quality factors or attributes:

⋄ Reliability
⋄ Usability
⋄ Maintainability
⋄ Efficiency
⋄ Portability
⋄ Security
⋄ Flexibility

Different software systems also require different quality attributes to be emphasized. You would naturally expect "more" of the reliability attribute in a nuclear reactor control system than you would in a theatre-seat booking system. Similarly you would be surprised if a database in use by the Inland Revenue did not have more security than a database in use at a public library. Such attribute specifications must be explicitly captured during requirements analysis if the final product is to be delivered to an appropriate level of quality. Unfortunately, too often the process of requirements capture does not adequately address the quality requirements of the final system.

To try to reflect the complexities involved in the definition of quality the following definitions have now, almost universally, been adopted:

1. **Fitness for purpose**
   Does the software product do the job that it was intended to do? Does a piece of software actually address the problem that it was intended to address?
2. **Conformance to requirements**
   Does the software product do the job well? Assuming that the software that is delivered does fulfil the requirements that it was intended to fulfil, does it fulfil them well? Or does the software have

lots of bugs and faults in it? Does the software conform to things such as speed and reliability requirements?

Together these two statements constitute a definition of software quality. You cannot have quality with only conformance to requirements, as there is no point in having a perfectly fault-free system which is not the system that the user wanted. Nor can you have quality with only fitness for purpose; having a system that addresses the users' problems but has many faults is equally useless. Neither quality definition is more important than the other.

9.2.4 What is quality certification?

Quality certification is the external certification of an organization's SQM (the specific components of which are discussed in Section 9.3). In effect a quality certification scheme provides an organization with a standard Quality Management System (QMS) template. The detail of an organization's QMS will be specific to that organization, determined by that organization itself, rather than by the certified scheme. A certified QMS is aptly described by Cameron Low when he says that the TickIT scheme is:

> ... a suggested way of ensuring that the things are done in the way that it has been decided that they should be done. It does not prescribe how they should be done [Low, 1990].

Bodies such as the British Standards Institution (BSI) and the International Standards Organization (ISO) have traditionally devised external quality schemes, although the Department of Trade and Industry (DTi) has delved into this area recently to produce the TickIT scheme (with good results). The usual quality schemes that are implemented by software-producing organizations are:

◇ The ISO 9000 series (International)
◇ The EN 29000 series (European)
◇ The BS 5750 series (British)
◇ TickIT (DTi)

Until comparatively recently most of these certificates were not software specific, but were generally applicable to any organization which either produced a product or delivered a service. Consequently these quality systems had only limited use to the software industry. Fortunately, the newer quality certification schemes do specifically relate to software development (for example the TickIT scheme and ISO 9000-3).

There is not a great deal to choose between any of the generic schemes, indeed the older schemes (such as BS 5750 and ISO 9001) are effectively identical. They all include the following broad requirements:

◇ Product identification and traceability
◇ Document control
◇ Inspection and testing
◇ Control of non-conforming products
◇ Design control
◇ Internal quality audits

There does seem to be an element of confusion concerning external quality certification, as many people refer to such schemes as quality "standards". Indeed that is what they are — standards for Quality Management Systems. They cover the whole framework of the development process, rather than any specific individual part of it. The confusion seems to arise when it is assumed that because things like BS 5750 are standards, they will automatically contain all of the other standards for all areas of software development. This is not the case. Quality standards do not, for example, include standards for producing C language code. Nor do they include standards for producing a User Guide. These kind of standards are specific operational standards. They relate to specific areas of the software development process and are usually specific to particular implementation environments. Such operational standards do not relate to the development process as a whole. It is, however, likely that a QMS will include a variety of these operational standards. Indeed it is exactly these kind of operational standards that an organization will develop for themselves as part of the QMS customization process.

9.3 Mechanisms for software quality

9.3.1 Introduction

Throughout history, organizations have been able to produce goods which are of good quality without fussing about Quality Management Systems or bothering with quality certification. However, most of these organizations tend to be skill-based which produce handmade one-off items.

The problem today is how to get a good level of quality in an ordinary commercial environment, rather than just in a special handmade environment. This challenge is especially relevant to software developers as users demand more and more software, and software that is increasingly sophisticated but at low prices. Software purchasers basically want mass-produced Rolls-Royces at Ford Escort prices!

The rest of this section concentrates on the issues and mechanisms that organizations wishing, or needing, to improve the quality of their software must address explicitly. Most of the mechanisms discussed here can be applied to many different industries and must be customized to specific industries like software development. This section also discusses such customization; it discusses the importance of a quality improvement culture together with a process-orientated view of software development. It also describes the components of a SQM.

9.3.2 What is a "quality improvement culture"?

When an organization tries to improve software quality it is vital that all its staff (at all hierarchical levels) have a commitment to improving the process of software production. All too often, organizations seem to have a commitment only to implementing a SQM and gaining quality certification. Quality mechanisms and formal quality systems are pointless without this underlying improvement culture. Everyone within an organization sees particular areas of suboptimization and this knowledge must be systematically captured in order to allow that organization to improve effectively. Many improvement culture ideas come directly from the notion of Total Quality Management and from the Japanese notion of "Zero Defects". Creating such a culture includes:

◇ Setting up mechanisms for encouraging staff to suggest how things can be improved and rewarding people for making those quality improvement suggestions.

◇ Making all staff aware of the benefits that improving quality will bring to them and to the organization.

◇ Training staff in any new working practices.

◇ Introducing the idea of internal *Quality Chains*. That is, the notion that all departments or sections have their own internal customers and in turn are customers to other internal departments.

◇ Introducing non-threatening improvement forums, such as *Quality Circles* (where a Quality Circle is simply a group of workers who meet together, preferably off-site, specifically to discuss how procedures can be improved).

While sounding straightforward, these are difficult cultural changes for an organization to make and many organizations fail to tackle this fundamental issue.

The rallying of staff to point out the ways in which things could be done better is crucial to the success of a quality improvement programme. Often it is tackled via a suggestion scheme of some sort — although all too often suggestion schemes are implemented so poorly that they are doomed from the start. A doomed suggestion scheme, and there have been plenty of them, usually has at least one of the following characteristics:

1. In the worst case, some suggestion schemes allow the situation where a suggestion (whether beneficial or not) that is unpopular with management will be held against the person making the suggestion. Clearly people are going to be wary of making suggestions in these circumstances, although they may make suggestions that reinforce existing management views.
2. A frequently encountered suggestion scheme simply pays lip service to the suggestions that it receives. Such a scheme will usually give many reasons why any suggestion cannot possibly be implemented. It basically ignores the suggestions that it receives. Clearly people will not waste their time making suggestions in these circumstances.
3. A common suggestion scheme scenario is one where the people who make the suggestions are then given the (additional) task of implementing that suggestion. Getting extra work is not usually a good motivator for making a suggestion.
4. The person with the suggestion may think that their suggestion is likely to make people redundant. Again most people would not make such a suggestion.

The above are common manifestations of suggestion schemes, and are all culturally damaging. Any initiative which tries to release the knowledge and experience of employees as to where an organization could do better must be genuine in its desire to see real improvement. Sometimes this will mean that some people in an organization will not like the means by which improvements can be made. Improvement initiatives must also be supportive of participants, and not threatening, as people are perceptive to hidden agendas.

9.3.3 What is all this software process business?

A process-based view of software development is essential to any organization's ability to improve software quality. Thinking of quality only in terms of the immediate software product is like locking the stable door after the horse has bolted. It is the process by which the product was produced that effected the final product's quality.

A process is the means by which anything is done or any activity performed. The development of a piece of software has a process, as does the making of a cup of tea. Typical examples of software development process elements include:

⬦ Systems Analysis
⬦ Design
⬦ Inspecting and reviewing
⬦ Writing documentation
⬦ Testing

Each of these elements will also be processes in their own right. So, for example, constructing a design will include selecting appropriate algorithms, designing the system's overall structure, consulting the analysts and so on. Each process element also has resource inputs and product outputs. For example:

Process:	Writing documentation
Input resources:	n person-months, software tools (word processing software etc.), hardware (printers, PCs, copiers etc.)
Output products:	User manual, maintenance manual etc.

In order for a process to produce a quality product, the following three conditions must exist:

1. Explicit and measurable quality goals must be captured at the user requirements stage.
2. The process itself must be well understood and be formally defined.
3. The development process must be flexible enough to allow it to be continuously refined and improved.

Sounds straightforward, but many software producing organizations have none of these things. They do not capture the users' explicit quality requirements in a measurable way (this is discussed in more detail in Section 9.4), and so do not know what level of quality they are aiming for. They do not have a defined process of software development, instead they have an *ad hoc* process which is not written down. In short, such organizations have no control over their development process and so have no control over the quality of the products that the process is producing, nor can they hope to tune their development process in order to accommodate new or changing quality requirements. Studies suggest that 80% of organizations are currently in this state [Myers, 1993].

An organization producing high-quality software will be characterized by its ability to control software quality levels and the development process. Given initial quality requirements, the organization will not only be able to meet these requirements but be able to do so repeatedly. Its software development process will be predictable and repeatable. A constantly sound process will produce consistently sound software — although there is nothing to stop an organization consistently producing a bug-ridden product if it has a consistently poor process!

More importantly, an organization without a development process understanding will find it is almost impossible to locate the root cause of any faults that emerge at the end of the process. So if a fault is discovered in a piece of software during testing, although that specific fault can be repaired, it is difficult to pinpoint when the fault was introduced (specification, design, coding?) and why it got there. So it is likely that the same sort of fault will probably be introduced into the next piece of software that is developed.

In conclusion, the following quote is worth remembering:

> Good people do good work, but they do even better work within a process framework [Munson, 1994].

9.3.4 What is a Quality Management System?

The most successful organizations at producing high-quality mass produced goods are widely known to be Japanese. Japanese companies almost all operate rigorous Quality Management Systems. Whilst it is clear that many things have contributed to the success of Japan, it is generally agreed that the comprehensive use of QMSs by Japanese companies has contributed significantly to the success of Japanese industry. Now, an increasing number of successful software producers in the Western World also have formal Quality Management Systems. Prime examples of such successful companies are Hewlett-Packard, RACAL and Motorola. It seems that if an organization is to successfully improve its quality levels, in a mass-production environment, then a Quality Management System is essential.

Unfortunately, many organizations put a Quality Management System in place and do not introduce the essential precursors to such a system that is a quality culture and a process-based view of software development. A Quality Management System without such supporting structures is likely to have a negative effect on quality. If lots of quality mechanisms are put in place without everyone in the organization actively using them, then they become a resource drain rather than a resource liberator. Indeed it is depressingly common to see a Quality Management System that is simply an end in itself.

Quality Management Systems have three basic elements:

1. Quality controls
2. Quality assurance
3. Quality management

Quality controls

There will usually be specific controls at the end of each part of the development process to ensure that each sub-process has attained the intended level of quality. For example, code will be subjected to quality control at the end of the coding process. This will usually take the form of inspecting and testing the code. The kind of quality control mechanisms will, of course, differ according to the particular process that they are being applied to. But the basic aim of quality control is to ensure that the output product of one process (for example, the design product of the design process) is at the appropriate level of quality to become the input resource to the next process (for example, the design document will be an input resource for the coding process). Quality control measures will be carried out by the development staff themselves. Quality controls include:

1. Software inspections, reviews and walkthroughs
2. Software testing
3. The application of standards, procedures and checklists

Software inspections, reviews and walkthroughs

These are used to check process products for faults and non-conformance to standards and requirements. They will be applied to software components which range from specifications to test plans. Surprisingly, software inspections (formally implemented as *Fagan Inspections*) are a very effective means by which errors can be found and often prove better at finding faults than testing [Gilb and Graham, 1993].

Software testing

Testing is generally considered as one of the final arbiters in the determination of a piece of software's quality. Clearly, it is a major source of evidence regarding the number of faults in a software system. Consequently, testing is an important quality control mechanism, because the number of faults revealed during testing can be a good indicator of the quality of the development process and of the final piece of software.

However, the results from testing must be treated with caution. Such results do not always give a true indication of how good the development process was, nor of how good the software product is. Finding few errors during testing might just be a function of poor testing rather than of a good quality process and product. Furthermore, other verification techniques, such as inspection, may actually be far more effective at revealing software faults (as AT&T have discovered [Godfrey, 1986]).

It is also tempting to think that simply putting more effort into testing can improve quality. This is a short-sighted (though disappointingly common) viewpoint. Testing can never improve the actual development process; it can only reveal faults in the product.

The application of standards, procedures and checklists

Standards

Standards are essential to any QMS. They confirm in writing what any process product should be like when it is finished. There will usually be a range of operational standards which operate on products as diverse as:

◇ Documentation
◇ Specifications
◇ Designs
◇ Code
◇ Test plans

A documentation standard, for example, is likely to address aspects of documentation such as:

◇ Naming conventions
◇ Structure
◇ Presentation (fonts, size, highlighting etc.)

Procedures

Procedures are also essential to any QMS. They define, again in writing, how any part of the development process should be performed. Procedures can be applied to elements such as:

◇ Analysis
◇ Design
◇ Testing
◇ Providing user support

Checklists

Checklists are frequently used as supplements to standards and procedures. They are simply used as an *aide-mémoire* to actually applying standards and procedures. Checklists are useful during auditing.†

---

† Audits can be internal or external and are carried out to ensure compliance with a QMS. They are crucial to external quality certification.

Quality assurance

Ideally every software development will have its own quality plan. This plan will set out the criteria that are required by a specific development. It will also detail the controls that will be used to assure those levels of quality. The plan will be designed by the development team and the quality assurance staff together. At the quality assurance stage, compliance with that quality plan is assured. This means that checks are made to make sure that all of the controls in the quality plan have actually been applied. This stage is most effectively undertaken by independent quality assurance staff rather than by the development team. Clearly potential difficulties exist whenever external people check that any work has been done correctly or when the organization is an extremely small one. These problems are discussed in Section 9.4.

Quality management

The Quality Management System itself is a system like any other system, it has a process. Like any other process unless it is continually improved then it will stagnate and ultimately become obsolete. Consequently, it is at the quality management level of a SQM that the system itself is reviewed and improved. It is also at this stage that organizational-wide structures and strategies are devised. A Quality Manual usually documents this level of the QMS.

Finally, a rather useful way to think about a QMS is:

Say what you are going to do	=	Quality management
Do it	=	Quality control
Prove that you have done it	=	Quality assurance

9.4 The problems of introducing software quality mechanisms

9.4.1 Introduction

There are many problems associated with introducing quality practices into any working environment. Introducing quality practices can be a big organizational change and the impact of any organizational change is not to be underestimated. Furthermore, the special nature of the software product probably makes these problems even more acute. It is not surprising, therefore, that the negative points of quality are often over-emphasized by those in the software industry. The industry does not, on the whole, seem keen to change its ways. In an industry which is constantly changing to keep up with developments in technology, quality working practices are seen as an expendable change — one change too far perhaps?

Introducing a proper QMS is frightening and risky for an organization, particularly for the management of an organization. After all, if developers are to be encouraged to criticize the system in order to improve that system's ability to produce good-quality products, isn't that what managers were supposed to be doing anyway?!

It is also true that, to an extent, formal Quality Management Systems have not been the success that they were heralded to be. That is because many organizations have introduced a QMS for the wrong reasons — because they simply wanted quality certification.

It is also interesting, and probably significant, that managers seem to demand a high level of quantitative evidence to support the view that introducing quality working practices will be beneficial to the organization. Much more quantitative evidence, I suggest, than they demand in order to justify the introduction of an expensive new testing tool or a new PC network. This is rather ironic when one considers that it is just this kind of objective decision making that quality systems seek to promote. Humphrey has a relevant observation to make on this issue:

> When managers **don't** want something they ask for financial justification [Humphrey, 1989].

However, to make matters even worse it is also clearly evident that organizations who do have formal Quality Management Systems are reluctant to publish their experiences. This means that there is a frustrating lack of public domain data with which to thoroughly verify the long-term effects of introducing a Quality Management System. This lack of public data is probably due to four things:

1. The quality systems that are in place are still relatively new and it is too early for proper data to be available.
2. Organizations do not want to admit publicly to the real quality of their software — especially if it is bad.
3. Organizations do not want to lose their competitive edge by saying how successful their quality improvement programme has been — or everyone might start doing it.
4. Organizations do not want to lose market confidence by admitting to an unsuccessful quality programme.

This lack of willingness to publish results is worrying and paradoxical. Worrying in that, how are the quality problems of the whole industry going to be solved if organizations are reticent about publishing their own experiences? Surely the quality of our software, in many application areas, is now too important to leave developers to find out "the hard way" how to get it right? Paradoxical in that, trying to improve quality is all about learning from past mistakes and focusing on how things can be done better in the future, and if the industry as a whole is not willing to do this then how can it expect individuals within an organization to do it?

This section focuses on the perceived and actual problems that people, within the software industry, have about introducing a quality-driven approach to software development.

9.4.2 There is nothing wrong with the quality of the software that we already produce

Well, I wish you would tell us all how to do it! Anyway, how do you know? Where are your metrics to prove it?

9.4.3 Getting measurable quality goals is impossible

Difficult — yes; impossible — no.

A great deal of work has been done recently to try to introduce more rigor into defining quality goals. After all, if you do not have any initial quality goals there is no way that you can tell if you have achieved the right level of quality in the final product. Having quantifiable goals is imperative to an effective quality system. Indeed, not having quantified quality goals has been the downfall of a number of quality initiatives.

First, it is important that every separate development has its own model of quality. So that a unique pattern of quality attributes is defined for each development (see Section 9.2). Second, something similar to the Goal Question Metric model of Fig. 9.1 should be applied [Basili and Rombache, 1984]. This model applies a step-wise approach to the identification of the measurable attributes of a system that reflect the top-level goal identified.

In the following example (adapted from *The ami Handbook* [The ami Consortium, 1993]) with the goal of improving a product's reliability, it should be seen that the collection of historical data (metrics) on the development of software products is crucial to the improved development of present and future software products.

Goal		Improve product reliability
Question	1	Where are errors found?
	2	What type of errors are they?
	3	How much test coverage performed ?
	4	How much test effort?
	5	How much inspection effort?
Metric	6	Error location
	7	Interface error
	8	Initialization error
	9	Loop control error
	10	Percentage test coverage
	11	Test effort person-hours
	12	Inspection effort person-hours

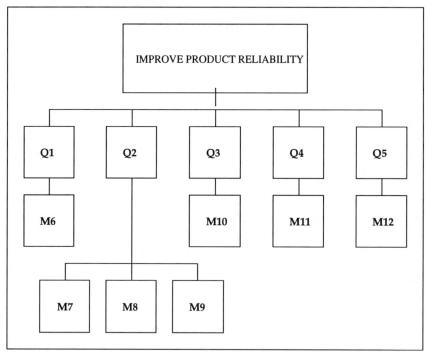

Figure 9.1 Goal Question Metric model

One of the problems with the identification of measurable goals is that people think such goals must always be absolutely objective. Clearly, having completely objective measures would be ideal, but such an aim is unrealistic. For example, defining goals related to usability is hard to achieve without knowledge of how people feel about a system. This can create difficulties, as sometimes an over-emphasis on strictly objective measures takes place, to the detriment of actually modelling the quality of an attribute. So, for example, if we modelled usability purely in terms of objective measures we would end up with an impoverished model. Such a model would concentrate upon measuring things like:

1. The length of time taken to learn how to use x function.
2. The number of mistakes made in y length of time.

Obviously, measuring usability only in terms of the above would not actually capture its true essence.

The important point about measurability is that, rather than only ever using objective measures, it is more important that the measures that are applied are planned in advance and are consistently applied.

9.4.4 Why do we need QA people? We can manage very well without them, thank you!

Independent Quality Assurance people are important as far as assuring that the things that were meant to be done were actually done. In other words: checking that quality controls were correctly applied and that those controls did the job for which they were intended. Having a person who is independent of the development process means that the assurance process is, theoretically, done on an objective basis; QA people are not under the same project pressures as developers to meet deadlines etc. The same argument has been accepted for software testing for a long time now. It is psychologically difficult and probably impossible to check your own work effectively. After all, no one actually wants to find errors in their own work.

However, even accepting that independent assurance is desirable and necessary does not detract from the fact that introducing extraneous people to check that everything is in order can present serious interpersonal difficulties. Developers (or anyone else for that matter) do not like having things checked by "outsiders".

Developers often resent QA people. They may feel that they can assure their work themselves (however, even with the best will in the world they cannot). They may also be unconvinced as to external QA peoples' qualifications or abilities for the job. Some of these concerns are valid. In the past it was not unusual for bad developers to be redeployed in QA roles. Obviously, assigning roles in this way is disastrous for the

QA function; furthermore, good people have not aspired to a QA role and again the QA function has suffered.

In short, although an independent QA function is essential, if it is to be effective it needs to be valued by the organization and the interaction between developers and QA must be managed sensitively.

9.4.5 We haven't got time to worry about quality systems — we are all too busy producing software

This is a cry I hear depressingly often. If organizations put more time into doing things properly in the first place they would not need to spend so much time on reworking errors and maintaining bad systems.†

In spite of this it is common to hear these "fire-fighting" cries. Indeed they illustrate very well that most of the software industry is operating on a short-term basis. A rather worrying trend when one considers how reliant the word is on good long-term computer systems.

9.4.6 Introducing a QMS would be far too expensive

For a small company it may well be. There is a high cost element to registering, administering and maintaining a comprehensive quality system, especially initially. Although special cut-down quality standards are now being developed for small firms (the TickIT scheme). It is probably also true that quality standards may not be as relevant to small firms as to large ones, as it is more likely that the development process is transparent to everyone, simply by virtue of the size of the process.

So far, the little evidence that there is suggests that the software producers which have introduced proper rigorous quality improvement programmes have improved on their ability to meet deadlines and have reduced their costs. However, many of the improvements brought about by a QMS are intangible and, therefore, difficult to define and measure. Setting up a quality system is obviously a significant investment,‡ but even that probably costs less than the total costs of introducing, for example, a large and complex CASE tool. However, the deciding factor is a cost/benefit analysis. When one considers how much effort is wasted in testing, re-working and maintaining software a QMS does not have to save very much money to be of actual benefit. Indeed as Crosby says:

> Quality is Free [Crosby, 1979].

---

† Maintenance is widely estimated to be consuming 70% of current total software development effort.

‡ Initial set up was estimated in 1988, by Price Waterhouse, to be in the region of £100 000 to £150 000 [Price Waterhouse Report, 1988].

9.4.7 Isn't a QMS just an exercise in paper generation?

Sometimes; although a successful QMS is not likely to be perceived as such. Paper-generating systems only pay lip service to the real aims of quality management. They are usually put in place either to gain "Brownie points" for managers or as a means to gain formal quality certification.

However, in order to get the best from a QMS, there will be more record keeping (only because practically no proper records are kept now though!). A certified QMS in particular introduces a certain amount of record keeping, but that is primarily for traceability purposes. A well-designed QMS will have transparently useful recording mechanisms and will not seem a pointless chore. Furthermore, organizations with good systems are also constantly refining the records that they do keep, to ensure that they only collect really useful and cost-effective data.

The fact that a number of quality systems have been said to be paper generation exercises suggests that software developers do not really like to take their own medicine. As whilst the software industry develops many systems for other industries to record and analyse operational data, it does not itself collect enough operational data. As a consequence of this lack of software development data the software industry has many operational and management problems. For instance, it finds it very difficult to manage the development process objectively, because there is usually no historical data on which to base decision-making. At an even more basic level, this lack of operational data means that software companies also find it hard to assess the effectiveness of particular tools and methodologies that they are using. Good record keeping has been practised for years in other industries: it is disappointing that the software industry is balking so much at the thought of keeping records itself. Imagine if the banking industry did not keep records for traceability and auditing!

9.4.8 But how are we supposed to be able to come up with our own QMS?

One of the biggest problems in implementing a QMS is the fact that quality mechanisms which work in one organization may not work in another. This means that each organization must, on the whole, devise the detail of its own system and getting these details right is difficult. It is easy to construct standards and procedures for the obvious things, but difficult to construct them for the right things. All too often I see standards for minutiae like the production of memos! Clearly it is very tempting to standardize the easy things, but unfortunately the easy things are not usually the important things.

As a consequence of the temptation to apply a QMS to easy things, some quality systems are an irrelevance to quality and a distraction to staff. Even more than that, however, such ineffectual systems can actually be destructive to quality. Quality Management Systems are not inert, they are not designed to be inert. Whether a quality system is good or bad, it will have an effect on the way in which things get done. If the system has focused on pointless minutiae then those minor tasks will adopt a vastly inflated significance. Quite rationally, staff will then spend more time doing the tasks that have been thus highlighted. Consequently, the things that really affect quality will be neglected.

9.4.9 Isn't quality just a silly attempt to mimic the engineering production line?

Quality is an attempt to take on board the good things from engineering that can be successfully used in software development. However, it is also about taking on board some of the good things from Management and Organizational Theory too. Software development is not so special that existing knowledge from other disciplines can arrogantly be ignored. Obviously, producing software is quite different from, say, manufacturing a car, particularly in the amount of individual skill and creativity that is still (and probably always will be) required to produce software. Also users do play a more direct, though often ill-defined, role in software development than they do in car manufacturing. Nevertheless, that does not mean, contrary to the belief of many software engineers, that software production is a law unto itself. Nor does it mean that software development should continue to be done in a totally unstructured and ill-disciplined way. Too often software developers seem to think that they have nothing to learn from other disciplines and other industries.

9.4.10 Aren't all these standards and procedures just a way to make everyone into a drone?

Software engineering needs individuals!

Standards and procedures have an undeservedly bad reputation. This is probably as a result of two things. First, the management of some organizations imposes standards and procedures on developers. If this is the case then they are probably doing so for reasons other than for improving quality. The usual reason is staff control. In such a situation it is hardly surprising that developers resent using these standards and are actively keen to see them fail. Second, some standards have been designed by the wrong people — not the people actually doing the job.

Obviously, such standards are just not useful to the people who *are* doing the job.

Standards and procedures are not about standardizing people, they are about standardizing the product. Good standards and procedures should liberate people, rather than standardize them. They will allow people to focus their individuality and creativity on the proper task in hand. All too often a good developer's valuable energy is wasted on deciding the most appropriate way of going about a development and on deciding its appropriate quality level. In effect, individual developers can spend a lot of time reinventing standards and procedures for every new development. Obviously, across the organization, this process can be very expensive.

Usually, you will find, people are secretly keen on standards and procedures and if there are none in use by the organization, they will develop and use their own personal (and often private) ones. The use of QMS allows developers simply to get on with the job, having already identified the most effective way of going about it. Of course, there may be some initial selection of the most appropriate standard for any particular development.

On the other hand, standards and procedures that do not address the real issues of software quality or which do not themselves evolve, will become irrelevant and dangerous. If they are too detailed they will break the simplest task down into many subtasks and become shackles rather than facilitators. Furthermore, a poorly designed QMS will quickly lead to an inflexible "more than my job's worth" attitude developing amongst staff. If staff are told how they must do absolutely everything, then that is all they will do and no more. Successful standards and procedures will have two characteristics. First, they will be devised by the staff who are actually using them. Second, they will reflect the working practices of the best and most experienced staff that are already doing the job. These good standards and procedures will prevent people having to learn how to do a job "the hard way".

9.4.11 Aren't today's quality standards just tomorrow's handcuffs?

This is a good point. Producing software is a creative activity. Maybe it will become less so as we have more practice at doing it, and as more developers re-use existing software components. Perhaps we don't have to reinvent the wheel every time we produce a new data processing system. Though admittedly the signs don't point to a reduction in creative input. Indeed, as user demands become more sophisticated maybe even more creativity will be required. The point is that it would be disastrous if the necessary creativity was straitjacketed out of software development.

A successful QMS will channel creativity and skill into improving the whole organization's ability to produce quality software. As I have said, developers will also be encouraged to improve the working practices of the whole organization. After all, it is the people on the ground who really know how they can be improved. So you could say that quality systems open up additional creative channels for developers rather than restricting creativity. I would go further and say that a good quality system liberates developers from the factory environment that I frequently see software developers working within.

However, if any QMS does introduce creative restrictions this is not a function of the QMS *per se*, but rather a function of poor management. Sorry, there is not much that I can usefully say about that!

9.4.12 Isn't quality certification just an attempt by professional bodies to interfere in things for their own ends?

So far, the least well-received part of introducing a Quality Management System is quality certification (Section 9.2). Ironically, it is also probably the most common reason for an organization to introduce a quality system at all. Many organizations find that the systems put forward by professional bodies are too vague and do not address many of the crucial quality issues. Maybe that just confirms what the software industry has long thought anyway — that all software development environments are different and it is unrealistic to try to provide a model that they can all use. Organizations are individual, and for the most part, need to work out what the best quality mechanisms are for them. Indeed, it is only relatively recently with the emergence of TickIT and ISO 9000-3 that quality certificates have even addressed software quality at all. BS 5750, for example, although popular amongst software developers seeking certification, is applicable to a wide range of product and service provision, including things like refuse collection services!

Probably the most damning criticism of the certificated systems is that they fail to address the cultural changes that are necessary for an organization to really improve quality. A number of organizations simply use BS 5750 to keep closer tabs on their employees — which is totally counter to any mature notion of quality improvement. In fact I believe that it is possible to introduce a certificated QMS and yet not improve software quality at all. Furthermore, such systems have been rightly criticized for being too bureaucratic, cumbersome and expensive to administer. These criticisms are, of course, especially relevant to small firms.

Increasing numbers of organizations seem to see introducing a certified QMS system as an end in itself, rather than a means by which to improve quality. Indeed I know of some organizations which are certificating an element of their operations, in one case their marketing section, and then implying certification for their software. I also know of an organization which is seeking certification, in an utterly minimal way, simply to retain financial backing from its bank. It seems to me that such systems are open to abuse and often do not address the real software quality problems anyway.

Although having said that most of the current quality certification schemes are disappointing, I do not believe that the professional bodies had dishonourable intentions when they formulated the schemes. Indeed the schemes do get better as time goes by (for example, TickIT being one of the better, and later schemes). I am sure that this continuous improvement of the schemes themselves will continue, although probably at a rather slower pace than the industry would like.

9.4.13 My software engineers won't put up with all this quality rubbish

Although senior staff often use this kind of statement as an excuse for delaying the introduction of a QMS, research suggests that ordinary members of the development staff are in fact keen to see the introduction of a QMS. They very much want to see quality improve and are enthusiastic about anything that might help this to be brought about. Paradoxically, it has also been suggested that it is the middle managers who are in fact most resistant to the introduction of rigorous quality working practices [Card and Glass, 1990]. This latter group of staff seem to have an inflated view of current software quality and, as a result, do not see the need to introduce new working systems.

Furthermore, although many managers say that developers will not cooperate in a QMS, a major part of introducing a QMS is to actively encourage staff to improve the organization's internal working systems. I personally don't know anyone who does not have suggestions as to how the system that they work within can be improved!

So, contrary to popular belief, ordinary development staff are often keen on a more formal approach to software development — as long as they have been involved in devising any new working practices, and as long as those new working practices are seen to be useful. It is often forgotten that people actively want to do a good job. A QMS aims to allow people to work as effectively as possible and I think that this is what most people strive for as individuals anyway.

9.5 Conclusions — All this quality stuff sounds too good to be true!

Obviously, I am rather biased! Indeed some people would probably go further and say that I have too much of an idealized vision of quality, though I hope that I have not made it sound too easy, as implementing a successful quality system is most certainly not easy. It takes enormous commitment from the whole organization, as well as a significant capital investment. It also takes lots of initial bravery together with long-term improvement stamina. But the results from software organizations which have implemented quality systems are very encouraging. Clearly, focusing the creativity and skill of software practitioners on improving the way that software is produced is bound to pay dividends in the long run. However, too often when I speak to colleagues within software companies I get the impression that everyone is waiting for everyone else to implement a proper quality system. No one really wants to be in the first tranche. An example of the software industry not wanting to take its own medicine, I wonder? We don't hesitate very much when it comes to developing the first object-oriented client database or the first artificially intelligent personal loans system! Maybe it is time that the industry got its own house in order.

Most of the ideas surrounding software quality management have been around for many years. For the most part the ideas are an established part of business management and of engineering practice. However, I am frequently horrified at the whispered sneers and dismissive comments that I hear from people around me when I am, for example, listening to a conference speaker talking about some aspect of software quality management (typically something revolutionary like involving the developers in devising a quality plan!). These people, I hasten to add, are not usually junior members of staff either. Clearly, such attitudes do not bode well for improving software quality in the future. Such people still seem to believe that some miraculous new design methodology or CASE tool is bound to be developed that will to do the trick, or with a bit more effort in testing everything would be fine, or even worse (and perhaps even more common) that they will do it right next time anyway! Some people never seem to learn.

I do, however, take heart from the fact that because the software industry is beginning to mature, it will inevitably migrate towards the established quality practices that it sees successfully working in other areas.

About the author

Tracy Hall is a senior lecturer in Software Engineering at the University of Westminster. She previously lectured for a number of years at Staffordshire University.

Whilst trying to develop good quality software, Tracy finds that wearing a suit is just about as useful as most CASE tools or SQA without proper commitment. Although they may give the impression that a good job is being done, they do not actively contribute to the task in hand, and may well be embarrassing examples of the "Emperor's New Clothes".

References and further reading

Godfrey A. (1986), *AT&T Technical Journal (whole issue)*, AT&T, 65(2) March 1986.

The ami Consortium (1993), *The ami Handbook*, South Bank University.

Basili V. and Rombache H. (1984), *A Methodology for Collecting Valid Software Engineering Data*, IEEE Trans on Software Engineering, Nov. 1984.

Berry D. (1993), *Quality Management*, NCC/Blackwell.

Card D. and Glass R. (1990), *Measuring Software Design Quality*, Prentice Hall.

Crosby P. (1979), *Quality is Free*, McGraw-Hill

Daily K. (1992), *Quality Management for Software*, NCC/Blackwell

Gilb T. and Graham D. (1993), *Software Inspection*, McGraw-Hill.

Gillies A. (1992), *Software Quality — Theory and Management*, Chapman and Hall.

Jones C. (1994), *Software Management: The Weakest Link in the Software Engineering Chain*, IEEE Computer, May 1994.

Humphrey W. (1989), *Managing the Software Process*, Addison-Wesley.

Kitchenham B. (1989), *Software Metrics*, in [Rook, 1989].

Low C. (1990), *TickIT — Progress and Plans*, Software Quality Workshop.

Munson J. (1994), *Achieving Quality*, IEEE Computer, March 1994.

Myers W. (1993), *Debating the Many Ways to Achieve Quality*, IEEE Software, March 1993.

Price Waterhouse Report (1988), *Software Quality Standards: the Costs and the Benefits*, DTi.

Rook P. (1989), *Software Reliability Handbook*, Elsevier.

Sanders J. and Curran E. (1994), *Software Quality 'A Framework for Success'*, Addison-Wesley.

CHAPTER TEN

SOFTWARE INDUSTRY STRUCTURE OR CHAOS

BY TERRY TWOMEY

10.1 The professional view

The 1990s have witnessed progress in the UK software market by foreign suppliers, without a corresponding improvement in the position of the indigenous software industry. Analysis by the Department of Employment of the economic environment in the 1990s concluded that:

> what will distinguish successful businesses — and countries — from the rest is how effectively they use the skills and abilities of their people to meet the needs of the market and how quickly they respond to new pressures [Pearson *et al.*, 1988].

Now that the software industry has matured into a capital-intensive, international industry, with fewer opportunities for small companies, the cost and pace of technological development are proving problematic for the relatively small UK companies.

This chapter examines the software industry as it relates to the software engineering profession. Issues which impinge on the work of the software engineer are explored. Attempts to model the structure of the industry and how the software engineer is perceived to fit within that structure are addressed.

The controlling body for the computing profession in Britain, The British Computer Society (BCS) defines software engineering in their Industry Structure Model (BCS-ISM) as:

The function of combining investigative, analytical and design skills with an appropriate knowledge of hardware and software technology to define, design, construct, test, deliver and modify properly engineered information systems containing software as the major component [BCS, 1991].

Whilst there may be a sense of unreality about the BCS-ISM it remains the most comprehensive model available, concerning professional standards, skills requirements and training for the software professional. Hence it will be discussed here in some detail.

10.2 Software industry overview

This section looks at the current state of the world software market and the position of the British software industry within this market. The difficulties facing the software engineer within British industry are presented in Section 10.3, highlighting the need for a professional framework.

10.2.1 The world software market

The world software market was estimated to be worth $40 billion in 1985 [ACARD, 1986] and has continued to grow in value. The USA remains the leading market and production centre for software and hardware, with total computer revenues growing to 12.5% of its Gross National Product in 1990. Advanced countries, such as Japan, France and the UK, play a lesser role; while newly industrialized countries, including Singapore, India, China, Taiwan, Korea and Brazil, are striving to establish their place in the market. Other European countries that have made some progress on the world market include Germany in the area of packaged software and Sweden in telecommunications systems.

Holding approximately 70% of the world market, the USA has primary position in the software industry. Its leadership of the hardware market, a strong entrepreneurial culture and a large internal software market have assisted the development of the software industry in the USA.

France holds second place in the world software market, being the leading supplier in Europe and a strong presence in the USA. A history of clear government policy and support [Nora and Minc, 1980], twinned with an export-oriented commitment, has helped the French software industry to maintain its position in a highly competitive market.

Although a late entry to the software industry, Japan is exerting a growing influence. Software engineering was a weakness of Japan for a long time, but software productivity and quality is now high. Through partnership with the Japanese government in research and development, clearly targeted market sector penetration and a commercial philosophy geared to delivering quality, image and competitive pricing, Japan's position looks good for long-term development, [Kaminuma and Matsumoto, 1991]. An important factor in Japan's newly gained success has been a programme of secondment of top researchers from industry into national research projects.

10.2.2 Position of the United Kingdom

The UK software market accounts for 5% of the world market. UK firms hold 3% of the world market — about half that held by France or Japan. This share is made up of two components, with the UK holding close to 50% of the domestic market and 0.5% of the remaining world market. An estimated 7% of UK-produced software is exported, with the resulting imbalance in software imports and exports continuing to make a deficit contribution to national trade. The domestic software industry showed great promise in the late 1960s and throughout the 1970s, with the creation of many new, rapidly growing software companies. Throughout the 1980s the UK software market grew at an average annual rate of *circa* 20%, with a similar growth rate in the European market as a whole [Pearson *et al.*, 1988].

As the industry matured, UK software companies experienced increased competition from overseas competitors. In particular, IBM(UK) stands out as by far the largest competitor, with a turnover close to that of the rest of the UK software industry. Many American-owned multinational companies operate directly in the UK, including DEC, Hewlett-Packard and Wang and a significant number of products sold in the UK by software supply companies are imported from the USA.

Possibly the major reason for the decline in domestic success is the highly fragmented nature of the UK software industry. Because of their relatively small size, UK software houses, such as Hoskyns, Logica and Scicon, have difficulty competing with large multinationals.

To overcome this difficulty one of the strategic objectives of the Alvey Programme was that the UK should become a world leader in software engineering technology by the end of the 1980s [Alvey Committee, 1982]. This important objective has not been achieved to any significant degree. It could be argued that the Alvey Programme was too influenced by academia and has failed to serve the needs of UK industry. Whatever the reason for the failure to meet strategic objectives, the position of the indigenous software industry has become precarious in the 1990s.

10.3 Difficulties facing UK software engineers

The IT profession in the UK grew rapidly from 200 000 in 1985 to 230 000 in 1987, and more slowly to 270 000 in 1993. Of the latter, 40% (108 000) can be classified as software engineers in its widest sense.

The decline in growth in the 1990s, together with the uncertain nature of the industry, means that the above professionals are at risk. They are adversely affected in several important respects:

1. Lack of investment in training.
2. Limited career opportunities.
3. Threat of foreign takeover.
4. Challenge of rapid change.
5. Insecurity of tenure.

10.3.1 Lack of investment in training

Operating within tight financial constraints, the UK industry is notorious for its lack of investment in training. Software engineers need to keep up-to-date on the latest techniques and tools, which in turn requires an ongoing commitment to training. Given the current situation within the industry it is not uncommon to find software professions committing their own time and money to improving their skills.

10.3.2 Limited career opportunities

Closely allied to inadequate training is the lack of opportunity for development within an industry that operates largely on home ground and has an insular view of the software engineering world. Compared to their counterparts in American, French and Japanese companies, UK software engineers have fewer opportunities to broaden their horizons by working in corporate subsidiaries around the world, or by moving periodically into Research and Development projects. This situation is exacerbated by a recent build-up of staff in senior grades with insufficient recruitment to maintain a healthy stock of junior staff.

10.3.3 Threat of foreign takeover

Software professionals face the ongoing uncertainty of working in an industry prone to takeover by foreign competitors. For those who survive the shake-out that invariably follows such acquisitions, the future is often bright. However, the prospect of such a shake-out, and the uncertainty of working for an organization with an alien philosophy and culture, adversely affects the UK software professional's sense of confidence and initiative.

10.3.4 Challenge of rapid change

Continual and rapid change is a feature of software engineering that has proved problematic for the UK industry. Generally, the management of change has been poor, with the software industry being slow to respond to variations in market conditions. For example, as packaged software grew to dominate the software market in the 1980s, the UK industry continued against the market trend to concentrate on the production of bespoke, integrated systems.

As a result of the apparent inability to manage change, the UK industry continues to experience skill shortages at all levels. Lack of investment in training and the introduction of new skills results in periodic skill shortages, with the current shortage in graphical user interface design skills being the latest in a long series of skill shortages that have hindered the development of the industry.

10.3.5 Insecurity of tenure

The last decade has seen an increasing tendency to contract out software development and other IT needs of user organizations to IT services firms. In recent years this tendency has extended to complete external management of the entire IT function.

As the range of specialist services offered by IT expands, it is not surprising that the role of the specialist IT services firms has become more central. Hence, much of the recent growth in the software engineering profession has been in software houses and consultancies servicing the user companies.

In addition to subcontracting IT work, the employment of contract staff remains widespread. The percentage of employers subcontracting some of their IT work to individuals or to organizations was 42% in 1985, rising to 72% in 1987 [Pearson et al., 1988]. The extensive use of contract staff and the virtually permanent subcontracting of IT work are now well-established practices. The trend within IT user organizations is to maintain a core in-house group for support and policy development while contracting out much of the software engineering function. This approach has proved a cost-effective way of acquiring high-level specialist skills for short periods and specific projects. If it is extended as a means of hiring short-term computing staff for non-specialist functions, then it may backfire, resulting in ill-feeling amongst permanent staff working alongside contractors with no long-term commitment to the company but earning higher pay for the same type of work.

10.4 The BCS-ISM

In response to the needs of the software industry and the profession, the BCS has devised an Industry Structure Model for computing (BCS-ISM).† This section evaluates relevant portions of the software engineering substream of the BCS-ISM model.

The BCS-ISM scrutinizes professional standards, including training and development requirements of the various subsections or streams within the computer industry. It represents the detailed guidance provided by the official representative body of the computing profession in the UK, the British Computer Society. The BCS-ISM has been accepted as the basis for the European Informatics Skills Structure (EISS) [BCS, 1993].

The variation in skills requirements in different contexts, coupled with the divergence in software engineers career progression, reduce the value of laying down requirements in absolute terms. More general guidelines on the different areas and levels of knowledge and skill, however, may help to clarify the scope of learning requirements. The BCS-ISM attempts to provide a set of guidelines.

10.4.1 Entry and capability requirements

The model structures the software engineering profession into a hierarchy with seven distinct levels and includes guidance on entry requirements, capability requirements, and appropriate training and development at each level.

Level 1

On entry to the profession, an individual must either:

1. Be a graduate with an interest in Information Systems, basic keyboard skills and some exposure to the discipline of computing; or
2. Have a minimum of two years' relevant work experience with an aptitude for systems work.

The software engineer should be capable of:

◊ Assisting with system specification
◊ Converting a limited part of a logical specification into a more detailed physical design.

---

† © BCS, 1991. Extracts reproduced by permission.

◇ Constructing or modifying, testing, correcting and documenting simple program modules from detailed specifications.

◇ Interpreting and executing defined test plans of limited scope, in a thorough and reliable manner.

◇ Working with colleagues and users to install a fully tested software system in a user environment, incorporating any required revisions to manual and clerical procedures.

Level 2

On entry to Level 2 the software engineer should have achieved one of the following:

1. At least six months' satisfactory performance at Level 1 of any systems development role.
2. At least one year's Information Systems experience in another stream of the ISM.
3. A relevant degree-level qualification including substantial practical systems development work.
4. At least two years' experience in systems work, and a completed recognized training programme to prepare students for systems work.

Above-average inter-personal skills and the ability to put people at ease are also necessary.

At Level 2 the software engineer must be capable of performing some of the following tasks:

◇ Work with colleagues and users in carrying out investigation of requirements, analysis modelling and system specification.

◇ Be aware of and take account of any limitations of the target implementation environment and external interfaces.

◇ Convert a limited part of a logical specification into an appropriate physical design.

◇ Construct or modify, test, correct and document moderately complicated program modules from specifications.

◇ Construct, interpret and execute test plans of a limited scope in a thorough and reliable manner.

◇ Participate in system installation.

Level 3

On entry to this level, an individual requires one of:

1. One year at Level 2 in a systems development role.
2. Two years at Level 2 in another ISM stream.
3. A relevant research degree.
4. At least three years' work experience, with good understanding of commercial practice and an aptitude for systems work.

In addition to the tasks identified at lower levels, the software engineer at Level 3 should be able to:

◇ Verify requirements using appropriate techniques (modelling, proving, prototyping).
◇ Convert a logical specification into an appropriate physical design.
◇ Develop complex program modules from specifications.
◇ Construct, interpret and execute test plans.
◇ Practise techniques for achieving quality throughout the software development lifecycle.
◇ Within a supervised framework, take into account safety issues.
◇ Be familiar with relevant software and hardware.
◇ Use technical manuals.
◇ Take full responsibility for the scheduling, quality and timeliness of one's own work and to guide less experienced colleagues.

Levels 4 and 5

The entry and capability of Levels 4 and 5 are quite similar and form a natural progression from Level 3. Both require at least two years' satisfactory performance at the previous level or significant experience within another ISM stream.

Practitioners at these levels must have proven ability in the areas of essential competence appropriate to problem solving within a software engineering context, and good overall understanding of the breadth of Information Systems applications and practice, with in-depth knowledge of at least one area of specialization. In addition, they must have been involved in all major stages of software development projects.

Level 6

Entry to Level 6 requires one of:

1. At least two years' satisfactory performance at Level 5 in a development role.

2. At least eight years' Information Systems experience, with at least two years at Level 5 in another ISM stream, including a significant software development component.

The software engineer at Level 6 must be capable of:

◇ Taking full and ultimate technical responsibility for carrying out all stages of the software development lifecycle, including all technical policy decisions.
◇ Advising on and implementing quality control and assurance techniques and procedures for software development.
◇ Rapidly envisaging and outlining system options to satisfy user needs and to assess costs and the viability of alternatives.
◇ Researching and understanding the implications of new hardware and software without needing to learn detail.
◇ Advising on and justifying hardware and software policies, and technical standards, methods and procedures for general applicability.

Level 7

On entry to this ultimate level, the software professional must possess the equivalent of:

at least two years' experience at Level 6, together with clear evidence of exceptional knowledge in all matters pertinent to the technical areas of computer systems development. As a practitioner one must have held ultimate technical responsibility for at least two large or complex projects that have been successfully delivered, and have authoritative, widely recognized and accepted knowledge in a specific area of technical specialization or application area.

The software engineer at this level must be capable of:

◇ Taking ultimate responsibility for technical decisions covering a major unit of computing activity, including multi-site or multi-project groups.
◇ Taking responsibility for the engineering quality of systems produced within one's scope of authority.
◇ Assimilating rapidly the complex inter-relations between hardware and software and user's needs, giving sound advice and valid estimates of a system's likely behaviour and performance.
◇ Taking a lead in recognizing and promoting new opportunities for effective use of Information Systems or other related new technology.

◇ Designing, developing and implementing novel and successful tools or techniques relevant to some aspect of Software Engineering.
◇ Working with senior management in formulating policy and procurement decisions applicable to all areas of Information Systems, one requires the ability to write and speak fluently on all aspects of work and communicate effectively with all levels of management and in public forums.

10.4.2 Requirements versus reality?

In addition to the extensive list of capabilities above, from Level 1 a software engineer is required to show an awareness of quality issues, display a rational and organized approach, and demonstrate the ability to work in a team, carrying out the required reporting procedures. It is hard to imagine how a young novice software engineer can be expected to satisfy all of these capability requirements within two years of graduation.

Requirements such as "above-average inter-personal skills and the ability to put people at ease" at Level 2 are, in our opinion, too intangible and difficult to evaluate to be of much use as entry requirements. An attempt to apply these entry requirements to a selection of software engineering colleagues proved extremely difficult; producing, at best, questionable results.

By Level 2, one must be aware of the full lifecycle for software development and have an appreciation of the need for and means of achieving quality throughout the lifecycle. Moreover, an understanding of the need for software to exhibit attributes of any properly engineered system, such as fitness for purpose, reliability, efficiency, security, safety, maintainability and cost effectiveness, is required. The ability to use technical manuals for reference and to document all work to the required standard are essential. A software engineer at Level 2 should show an aptitude for becoming effective and persuasive in presenting technical problems, processes and solutions, both orally and in writing. The ability to plan and schedule one's own work within a limited time horizon is expected at this level. At this point even an experienced software engineer may begin to feel the pressure of meeting these somewhat intangible and over-ambitious capability requirements.

On attaining Level 5 some area of specialized knowledge, though not required, is expected. One must be seen to take a leading role in proposing technical solutions within one's expertise and scope, and show mature understanding of the relationship of the specialization to the product and the project as a whole.

Where specialized knowledge is offered at Level 6, one must be considered an expert and be capable of advising on the wider implications of its application. The ability to write and speak fluently on all aspects of work and communicate effectively with all levels of management is essential. One should also be in a position to plan and give technical short courses as required.

It would appear at this point that the term "software engineer" is being used to describe a superhuman who, along with being a professional with considerable computing expertise, is also adept at business management, public relations and communications, and indeed has somehow acquired the skills necessary to develop and deliver training courses. Surely the flaw in this profile is immediately apparent to all — there is nothing to indicate that the individual in question should hold a first-aid certificate!

Little can be said regarding the wish list of expectations at Level 7.

Whilst acknowledging the valuable contribution made by the BCS-ISM to the software engineering profession, a worrying assumption appears to underpin this hierarchy of capabilities. It seems that as one progresses through one's career in software engineering, in addition to acquiring new skills and training, all previously acquired skills and knowledge are assumed to be retained. Thus, as an individual moves through changing roles as a programmer, systems analyst, team leader, project manager and information resource manager during their working life, the implication is that all prior learning and skills remain relevant. The reality of rapid change in the computing and business world indicates otherwise.

10.5 Possible BCS-ISM enhancements

The BCS-ISM represents a serious attempt to model a dynamic, evolving industry. While this effort is appreciated, the result is somewhat unrealistic. It does not reflect the current situation in industry, assuming a development hierarchy rather than a continuum and ignoring the trend towards specialization within a maturing profession.

The primary purpose of the BCS-ISM is to offer a comprehensive structure model of the computing industry. In so doing it falls between two stools in terms of content. It is too complete to be merely a set of non-prescriptive indicators, while lacking the depth and added value of explicitly addressing the major concerns of the industry within the structure. The level of detail on capability and training requirements allows the model to be presented as an answer to many of the industry's problems. Yet in structuring the software engineering profession, key issues, such as quality of product, are not considered.

Neither is there any indication in the model of the reasoning behind the specification of levels such as the seven levels of software engineering. One can only hope that it has real significance, and is not merely a legacy of the long-outdated hierarchical view of management, which has little relevance in the interdependent, team-oriented context of software engineering. Without a clear statement of the rationale underpinning the BCS-ISM, its usefulness is difficult to evaluate.

Is the model realistic? Does it meet or anticipate the needs of industry, or is industry structuring the purpose in itself? Are capabilities and training requirements what software engineers want? Are the needs of the UK computing industry the same as those of other countries? Should software engineers be considered as individuals with very similar capability and development requirements, or as quite distinct participants in a group activity involving a wide range of skills and needs? To be authoritative in any meaningful sense an industry structure model should address such questions.

The need for a unified and definitive computer industry structure model has been obvious for some time. Unfortunately, the BCS-ISM and other models seem to have missed their target. As a result, several manufacturers, including Microsoft and Novell, have developed their own training and certification programmes.

10.5.1 Skills requirements

It is clear that different types of training requirements, such as training in technical, commercial and social skills, are being presented in the BCS-ISM. There is no attempt, however, to distinguish between the various types. Whilst the training and development guidelines given are useful as general indicators of requirements, their value would be enhanced by tying aspects of training and development to specific capability and entry requirements.

One might expect to find common skills requirement terminology shared between the advertised needs of the industry and the BCS-ISM. However, it is not uncommon to read literature from industry, the profession and education which seems worlds apart in terms of language and content. Thus employers advertise for people with very specific skills, such as C++ programming or SSADM, whilst the BCS-ISM demands transferable skills such as customer orientation, interpersonal skills and commercial awareness. To be fair, in the long term these transferable skills are required and are frequently talked about by personnel managers but rarely mentioned in adverts.

More specifically, annual skills surveys show rapid change in the skills in demand at any particular time. For example, the requirement for skills in C++ and object-oriented development techniques has grown at a phenomenal rate in 1993–4; and the "Microsoft Environment", centred on Visual Basic, looks set for similar success in the PC context.

These changes indicate the continuing development of software engineering. The ten software engineering skills most in demand in 1990 and 1993 are shown in the following table, where brackets show the demand in 1990 [Evans, 1994].

1990	1993
COBOL	C (2)
C	UNIX (3)
UNIX	WINDOWS (44)
CICS	COBOL (1)
DB2	ORACLE (10)
VME	RPG400 (51)
VMS	LAN (24)
RPG3	INGRES (14)
MVS	SQL (33)
ORACLE	NOVELL (48)

Whilst there is no guarantee that these will be in demand at the end of the 1990s, it is worth repeating that none of these skills is mentioned in the BCS-ISM. In defence of the BCS-ISM one might respond that it is intended to be a general structure and is therefore void of specific product skills. Such a defence merely serves to underline the chasm that can emerge between the model and the industry it claims to represent. In the rapidly-changing computer world, one would expect the model to be updated regularly, and thus have the facility to cope with skill changes at the product skill level.

10.5.2 The Professional Development Scheme

The BCS Professional Development Scheme (PDS) provides a framework for the assessment of experiential learning within the workplace and individual support and guidance on training for career development. For detailed information on training, experience acquisition and career development the PDS is recognized as a reliable and authoritative source for IT professionals. The scheme is intended to provide the concrete link between the ISM and computing practitioners via individually prepared Career Development Plans, with the ISM "performance standards" serving as an external quality control mechanism for the scheme. More direct quality control can be administered through the IT Competence Statements for National Vocational Qualifications (NVQs), thus creating linkage between the BCS-ISM, the PDS and the NVQ frameworks. The PDS was welcomed by industry and has expanded rapidly since its inception in 1985. With vigorous development and promotion it has the potential to meet many of industry's needs [BCS, 1993].

The PDS claims to use the BCS-ISM to provide a quality control mechanism for experience and training assessment on an individual basis. In this respect, it could be used to bridge the gap between the broad strategic requirements of the software industry (as reflected in the BCS-ISM) and the specific needs of software companies and hence practitioners (as reflected in the computing press).

10.6 Conclusions

10.6.1 Structure or chaos?

In summary, the software industry continues to evolve rapidly. Constant development and change are characteristics of the industry that are likely to continue for the foreseeable future. This state of flux adds great complexity to the task of modelling the industry. Paradoxically, it is because of this complexity that structuring the industry is so important. It seems reasonable that the development of an industry structure model should be overseen by the BCS, as the computing profession's representative body. This, of course, requires input from every sector of the industry and belief in the role of the BCS.

An obvious danger is that the scale of the modelling task can result in a "macro" model, which is too general to be of use because it barely reflects the specific activities of its practitioners at the "micro" level. To gain wide acceptance, the BCS-ISM needs to relate more closely in both language and content to the skills that are actually used and the tasks that are actually performed.

Perhaps what is needed is a closer integration of the BCS-ISM with the more practical PDS, NVQs and corporate schemes. Without such integration, the BCS-ISM may become a white elephant — being the official industry standard but disregarded by personnel and training managers and ignored by software engineers.

10.6.2 Future prospects

Although a modified BCS-ISM may go some way to solving operational and tactical problems within the industry, it will not — nor is it intended to — solve the wider problems. It is necessary to incorporate the model into a broader solution, with links to the overall strategy of the industry and the economy.

Subject to a strategic policy decision at national level, and extensive financial support from central government, three routes remain open to the development of the UK software industry as a player on the world market:

1. Aggressive government investment in the international development of the UK software industry and marketing of UK software abroad.
2. Creation of a large UK-owned software company via corporate mergers and acquisition, to represent and protect national interests in software.
3. Development of mutually beneficial links with leading foreign companies to promote the interests of UK companies in the world market.

First, a strategic decision could be taken at national level to promote the UK software industry to play a leading role in the world market. Such a decision would require full government support and a major financial commitment. It might also involve a shift in emphasis, promoting the production of packaged software to complement an existing strength in the development of bespoke systems.

Second, there is what might be termed "the ICL option", to attain critical mass in terms of corporate resources and market share through a series of nationally supported corporate mergers within the domestic software industry. This option would serve to strengthen the UK market position in the short term and ensure at least the survival of one nationally owned company in the long term.

Alternatively, there is the "motor industry option" involving strategic mergers and agreements with foreign companies, to ensure continued UK influence in the world market through involvement with leading multinational corporations.

If none of these strategic options is actively pursued, then the UK software industry may well be swallowed up piecemeal by the major players in the international software industry.

How does this relate to the mere mortals who have chosen software engineering as a career? They may well be asking themselves if there will be a software engineering profession in the UK ten years from now. Ironically, while the loss of a nationally owned software industry undoubtedly has repercussions for the profession, the quality of software engineering in the UK ensures its value as a commercial asset. While a major national initiative to support the industry might initially have an unsettling effect on the profession, it would create greater certainty in the long term for the survival and growth of that profession. If, on the other hand, ownership of the industry is lost to foreign companies, the software engineering industry in the UK would most probably maintain its current world position, and might even experience some growth in the short term as its products gained greater market exposure. The long-term effects of foreign ownership are less predictable, as national considerations give way to purely economic and political decisions.

About the author

Terry Twomey is a senior lecturer in information systems engineering at the University of Westminster. In a previous existence he was involved in corporate training and so has the heritage of a suit which he is determined to wear on all occasions. Whether this will make him a better software engineer or more professional, he is uncertain, but it does look nice and keeps him warm in winter.

References and further reading

ACARD (1986), *Software: A Vital key to UK Competitiveness*, HMSO.

Alvey Committee (1982), *A Programme for Advanced Information Technology*, HMSO.

British Computer Society (1991), *Industry Structure Model*, BCS.

British Computer Society (1993), *Professional Development Scheme*, BCS.

Evans P. (1994), *Salaries and Skills Survey, 3/3/94*, Computer Weekly.

Kaminuma T. and Matsumoto G. (eds) (1991), *Biocomputers, the next generation from Japan*, Chapman and Hall.

Kim C., Westin S. and Dholakia N. (1989), *Globalization of the Software Industry: Trends and Strategies*, Journal of Information and Management, vol 17 no 4.

Nora S. and Minc A. (1980), *The Computerization of Society*, MIT Press.

Pearson R., Connor H. and Pole C. (1988), *The IT Manpower Monitor*, Institute of Manpower Studies.

CHAPTER ELEVEN

DISCIPLINE OR PUNISH: THE CRUELTY OF NOT TEACHING SOFTWARE ENGINEERING

BY MARK PRIESTLEY

> *I beg leave to throw out my thoughts and express my feelings, just as they arise in my mind, with very little attention to formal method.*
>
> **Edmund Burke**, *Reflections on the Revolution in France*

11.1 Introduction

When the term "software engineering" first came into wide use it was not intended to name an academic discipline. The purpose of the first conference on Software Engineering in 1968 [Naur, 1968] was to address the inadequacy of contemporary techniques of software development, the so-called "software crisis". It was recognized that many problems arose because the scale of the projects that were being attempted far outstripped the ability of people to manage and control such developments. Engineering was recognized to be a discipline that had successfully addressed the problems of constructing large artefacts, and the intention was to see how and to what extent the engineering approach could be adapted to help control the production of software. Since then, a large body of software engineering research and experience has grown up, and many universities now offer courses leading to qualifications specifically in software engineering, at both undergraduate and postgraduate level.

From the point of view of the software engineering industry, this should be encouraging. A characteristic of a mature engineering discipline is the existence of a consensus on the basic knowledge and skills of the discipline, or in other words, agreement about what should be taught to trainees. Typically, the education of an engineer comes in two phases: first, a period of academic study mastering the theoretical foundations of the subject, and usually culminating in the award of a degree or equivalent. This is followed by a period of apprenticeship when the application of the theory on industrial-scale projects is learnt. A relevant professional body will then usually certify the survivor of this process.

At the moment, the software engineering profession does not share these characteristics. In particular:

◇ There is no required, or even recommended, undergraduate qualification. Many computer science graduates get employment in software engineering but, on the other hand, many companies are keen to recruit non-computer science graduates and to train them on the job.
◇ Software engineering curricula are very diverse, and there is wide disagreement about what they should include.
◇ The certification of software engineers is barely developed. The relevant professional bodies are weak, and certification is not widely recognized in industry as a necessary prerequisite for a career as a software engineer.

It might seem, therefore, that establishing software engineering programmes in universities would be unequivocally seen as a good thing, and as a valuable way of focusing the subject and speeding its evolution towards the status of a mature engineering discipline. A significant number of people involved in computer science and software engineering education do not share this view, however. There is a significant weight of opinion arguing that specialized software engineering courses should not exist, or at least not yet.

This chapter examines the reasons for this seemingly paradoxical stance, and argues that although there are genuine concerns underlying the arguments of the sceptics, it is very valuable to have specialized software engineering courses. Some proposals about the content of software engineering courses are then considered and the chapter finishes with an examination of the relationship between software engineering education and industry. Before this, however, it is worth looking at some of the arguments that have been put forward about the nature of software engineering and its relationship to other engineering disciplines.

11.2 Does software engineering exist?

As is perhaps inevitable for a young subject, software engineering regularly attracts misunderstanding and controversy. For example, here is the eminent computer scientist Edsger Dijsktra on the subject, in a paper called *On the cruelty of really teaching computer science* [Dijkstra, 1989]:

> ... software engineering should be known as 'The Doomed Discipline': doomed because it cannot even approach its goal since its goal is self-contradictory. ... If you carefully read its literature and analyse what its devotees actually do, you will discover that software engineering has adopted as its charter, 'How to program if you cannot.'

Dijkstra's argument is based on a very personal view of what programming is, entailing amongst other things the belief that the task of writing computer programs is radically different from other practical and intellectual activities. His basic argument for this claim is the observation that the assumptions of continuity that we make about the behaviour of most materials and artefacts simply do not hold for software, which exhibits instead a radical discreteness. By "continuity" here is meant the property that small changes lead to small effects: for example, if I turn the volume control on my amplifier a small amount I can expect the volume of the output to increase by a correspondingly small amount. In general, however, software does not exhibit this property: very small changes to a program's code can have very large and drastic consequences. A classic example of this is NASA's first Venus space probe, which was reputedly lost because of the accidental omission of a single comma in the FORTRAN code written to control it. This story may be apocryphal, but it is not implausible.

Based on this property of the discreteness of software, Dijkstra argues that the mathematics appropriate to reasoning about software development is that based on logic and algebra, and not the classical calculus-based mathematics used by engineers in other disciplines. This is uncontroversial: there is very little evidence in the literature to suggest that anyone ever thought that adopting the term "engineering" to describe software production entailed adopting all the detailed techniques and theories used by other engineers. (A prominent exception to this would appear to be David Parnas, initiator of some of the most promising ideas in the theory of software engineering. In a paper [Parnas, 1990] whose eccentricity rivals Dijkstra's, he seems to be advocating a computing curriculum largely based on traditional engineering mathematics.)

More strongly, Dijkstra argues that programs are mathematical objects that can only be produced by means of a formal process resembling a particularly rigorous kind of mathematical proof. Revealingly perhaps, the process of teaching students to produce programs in this way is the "cruelty" referred to in the title of his paper. Further, Dijkstra clearly believes that such mathematical approaches are both necessary and sufficient to overcome the existing problems in large-scale software development. It is because software engineering attempts to address the problems of software development without adopting suitably mathematical techniques that he pronounces the discipline doomed.

The large-scale adoption of mathematical techniques in software development is often referred to as "formal methods". The proposal that this approach offers a foundation for software engineering is a radical one, and is examined in more detail later.

A more balanced view of software engineering is offered by Tony Hoare. In *Programming is an engineering profession*, he contrasts "craftsmen" and "professional engineers" as producers of artefacts.

Craftsmen, who flourished in "earlier times and less advanced societies", possess unusual skills which have been learnt by imitation, practice, experience and trial and error in the course of a long apprenticeship to an acknowledged master of the craft. A craftsman

> knows nothing of the scientific basis of his techniques ... cannot explain how or why he does what he does ... and yet works effectively, by himself or in a small team, and can usually complete the tasks he undertakes in a predictable time scale and at a fixed cost, and with results that are predictably satisfactory to his clients [Hoare, 1989].

A professional engineer, on the other hand, not only serves the long apprenticeship of the craftsman but precedes this by many years of formal study, covering the mathematical and scientific principles underlying his or her particular branch of engineering. As a result, engineers are equipped to give rational justifications of what they do, and are in command of techniques which allow very large projects involving many workers to be undertaken and successfully completed.

Hoare's purpose in drawing this comparison is to suggest that software development today has more in common with the craft model than the approach of the professional engineer.† By examining the transition from a craft-based industry to a mature engineering profession, however, we may begin to see ways in which we can hope to move towards a more satisfactory practice of software development.

---

† Given the references above to predictable time scales, fixed costs and satisfied clients in the craft model, even this may seem over-optimistic.

11.3 Putting engineering into software development

In *Prospects for an Engineering Discipline of Software*, Mary Shaw considers in more detail what would be required of a mature software engineering discipline. She begins with a critical examination of the current state of software engineering practice, describing the term "software engineering" itself as a "statement of aspiration" rather than as a description of an existing discipline. She goes on:

> 'Software engineering' is a label applied to a set of current practices for development. But using the word 'engineering' to describe this activity takes considerable liberty with the common use of that term. The more customary usage refers to the disciplined application of scientific knowledge to resolve conflicting constraints and requirements for problems of immediate, practical significance [Shaw, 1990].

The clear implication is that software development does not currently fit this description.

Shaw models the transition from a craft to a mature engineering profession as taking place in two major steps. First, demand for the product becomes sufficiently great to necessitate the introduction of large-scale industrial production rather than small, workshop-based enterprises. Establishing this larger scale of production involves codification of the techniques used, development of new techniques, and adoption of working practices applicable to the larger scale. The second step occurs when a science explaining the industrial practice emerges:

> The problems of current practice often stimulate the development of a corresponding science. There is frequently a strong, productive interaction between commercial practice and the emerging science. At some point, the science becomes sufficiently mature to be a significant contributor to the commercial practice. This marks the emergence of engineering practice in the sense that we know it today – sufficient scientific basis to enable a core of educated professionals so they can apply the theory to analysis of problems and synthesis of solutions [Shaw, 1990].

What stage has software engineering reached in this evolution? In Shaw's view, the introduction of software development methodologies in the 1980s marks the beginning of the transition from the craft stage to the commercial production of software. Colloquially, this is marked by the change of emphasis from "programming in the small" to "programming in the large". This transition has not universally taken place, however, and in many areas, and even in many commercial firms, craft models of production are still the norm. The science applicable to software development, on the other hand, barely exists, and only in very isolated cases are anything other than very informal techniques applied. Software engineering is therefore not yet a true engineering discipline, and at present is only emerging (slowly and painfully) from the craft stage. More optimistically, Shaw sees no reason in principle why a suitable scientific basis for software development should not in time emerge, and software engineering acquire the status of a mature engineering discipline.

11.4 Software engineering as a discipline

The relevance of the above discussion for education can be summarized in the following three points.

First, a characteristic of a "true engineering discipline" mentioned by both Hoare and Shaw is that a long period of formal education is a prerequisite for entering the profession. Assuming that software engineering aspires to be such a discipline, it is clear that university-level courses in software engineering will be required to provide this formal education.

Second, in the case of the established engineering disciplines the purpose of this education is to equip neophytes with the scientific knowledge that underlies the field. The fact that this education is carried out in colleges and universities rather than in engineering firms is an indication of the maturity both of the field (education is more than simply apprenticeship) and of the science, which can be separated out from its applications and taught as a self-contained body of knowledge.

In addition to formal education, of course, a period of apprenticeship is still required before recognition as a qualified engineer is granted. The important thing about this, however, is that it takes place *after* the formal training: what is being learnt is the application of the principles of the discipline, not the complete subject.

Third, as Shaw says, the scientific basis of software engineering has not yet been developed. We can teach isolated bits of theory and a variety of useful techniques, but there is little sign yet of any unifying, underlying science that could be applied to the task of engineering software systems.

There is a clear incompatibility here between the desire of the software engineering profession to have an extended, formal period of education leading to professional accreditation and the lack of scientific foundations for software engineering which might have been expected to form the major part of such an education. In its crudest terms, the dilemma for educationalists can be expressed as follows: if we have specialized software engineering courses, what are we to put in them?

In recent years, a vigorous debate has been taking place on this subject; a good source of material is the proceedings of the series of conferences on software engineering education run by the Software Engineering Institute of Carnegie Mellon University [Ford, 1988; Gibbs, 1989; Demiel, 1990; Tomayko, 1991; Sledge, 1992].

Participants in this debate tend to adopt one of the following positions:

1. Software engineering is too specialized a subject for undergraduate-level education. Undergraduates should learn computer science, and become specialist software engineers only at Masters or PhD level.
2. In principle, undergraduate courses in software engineering are a fine thing, but at the moment the subject is much too immature to define and support such courses. In the meantime, computer science courses should be "seeded" with elements of software engineering.
3. Despite the immaturity of software engineering, it is still sufficiently distinct from computer science, and the needs of industry sufficiently pressing, to make it worthwhile offering undergraduate courses in the subject.

Implicit in these positions is grave uncertainty about the relationship between computer science and software engineering. The first position, for example, clearly assumes that software engineering is best thought of as a specialism within computer science; the second position does not go so far, but does assume that, pragmatically, software engineering can successfully be taught as such a specialism. Only with the third position is there acknowledgement of the possibility of software engineering being a separate subject from computer science.

The position argued for in this chapter is that there is a clear need to offer specialized courses in software engineering alongside traditional computer science courses. Although the two subjects share an interest in the same technology, and although there will be considerable overlap between software engineering and computer science courses, we believe that the needs of the software industry and of future software engineers are best met by offering specialized courses in software engineering.

The first observation to be made in support of this claim is that it is not at all clear that a qualification in computer science is necessary to provide a solid foundation for software engineering. Software engineers clearly need a good appreciation of many aspects of computer science, but this can be gained in much less than the time available for a full honours degree, for example. Software engineering should therefore be viewed as a client discipline of computer science, not as a speciality within it. These claims are considered in more detail in the next section, which examines the content of computer science courses in more detail.

Not only is computer science not a necessary foundation for software engineering, it is not sufficient either. As with any engineering subject, the ethos of software engineering is highly practical, and oriented towards the development of complex artefacts in response to real-world needs. This practical orientation is sufficiently fundamental to make it necessary to emphasize it throughout an entire university course: there is not time to acquire it otherwise.

A personal anecdote may make this point more vivid. Several years ago, I taught a final-year option course entitled "software engineering" to a group of students who up to then had followed a fairly traditional computer science course, similar to the one outlined in the following section. In the short time available, it was not possible to attempt any large-scale project with the students: the course instead attempted to convey the ideas of information hiding and modular design, and to outline some methodology of software construction. The results were predictably depressing: the students found the more theoretical ideas "abstract" and "irrelevant", and having only had experience of small, simple programs could appreciate neither the need for nor the benefits of a formalized software development methodology.

The most important conclusion that can be drawn from this experience is that the "software engineering" approach to software development can only be appreciated by students who have had prolonged exposure to software systems of a significant size, and who have experienced at first hand the difficulties of developing such systems in an unsystematic manner. It takes a long time, however, to give students this experience, and in particular it is not possible to convey both the problems and the solutions within the scope of a couple of specialized modules, as adherents of the second position above would advocate.

Finally, it should be recognized that there is a range of pragmatic and strategic considerations which have led to the institution of software engineering courses. For example, some institutions have felt obliged to offer courses titled "software engineering" in order to prevent the phrase being misused by non-computing departments. In a bid to appropriate the term, engineering departments are prone to interpret it as meaning "software *for* engineering". In this context, establishing a software engineering course can be seen as a clear statement of belief that there is a science of software development, and also as an attempt to provide a focus for the development of such a science.

Yet accepting the need for software engineering courses makes the following question inescapable: while we are waiting for software engineering to attain maturity and identify its scientific basis, what material should (or shouldn't) be included in software engineering courses? The following sections consider some answers to this question. Section 11.5 considers the relationship between software engineering and computer science, and the extent to which computer science is relevant to the software engineering curriculum. Section 11.6 evaluates the claim that formal methods form a suitable scientific basis for software engineering. Section 11.7 then examines a detailed curriculum proposal for undergraduate software engineering courses.

11.5 Computer science and software engineering

From the summary of the debate about software engineering education in the previous section, it is clear that there is a widespread belief that it is quite appropriate for software engineers to follow what is basically a course in computer science. This section looks in more detail at the computer science curriculum in order to evaluate this belief.

The name "computer science" is, on the face of it, rather curious: it implies the existence of a discipline centred around a piece of technology, rather than on any fundamental intellectual principles. Cynics might argue that equally compelling subjects could be invented, such as "refrigerator science":† this would presumably cover all aspects of the construction and use of refrigerators, including electronics and cookery. Clearly, the coherence of computer science as a discipline has to be argued for.

A representative description of computer science may be taken from the report *Computing as a Discipline* [Denning et al., 1989] which splits the core of computer science into the following nine areas:

1. Algorithms and data structures.
2. Programming languages.
3. Architecture.
4. Numeric and symbolic computing.
5. Operating systems.
6. Software methodology and engineering.
7. Databases and information retrieval.
8. Artificial intelligence and robotics.
9. Human–computer interaction.

---

† This may not be a joke: given the way that higher education in the UK is developing, I would not put much money on the non-existence of such a course.

This list contains an impressive diversity of subjects, and taken at face value would seem to require considerable breadth of abilities and interest from the student. For example, a study of computer architecture (area 3) often requires at least an appreciation of digital electronics, whereas human–computer interaction (area 9) is based largely on practical applications of psychology.

Looked at more analytically, the list seems to conflate at least three subjects. Areas 1, 2 and 4 are concerned with the theory of computability and its applications, areas 3 and 5 with computer technology, and area 7 with information systems. The remaining areas are concerned with either the applications of computers or aspects of the use of computer systems.

In this chapter, however, we are concerned not with the status of computer science but with the role it should play in the education of software engineers. Any rigorous treatment of software engineering would be entirely contained in area 6, software methodology and engineering. Many of the other areas describe relevant knowledge: some areas, such as 1 and 2, are likely to be central in any software engineering course. Others, however, are either relevant only to particular application areas (such as area 8) or are areas where an appreciation of the constraints placed on the software engineer is all that is needed (area 3).

The conclusion of the last two sections, therefore, is that computer science as conventionally understood is neither a necessary nor a sufficient prerequisite for software engineering. There are significant areas of overlap between the two subjects, but it does not seem satisfactory to teach software engineering simply as an adjunct to a computer science course.

11.6 The formal methods research programme

In recent years, the belief that certain areas of mathematics form the appropriate scientific basis for the study of software has received a lot of attention. This position is often referred to as a belief in 'formal methods'. Many things in computing have been described as formal. The characteristic of the position under examination here is the emphasis on treating software as a formal, mathematical object, amenable to mathematical techniques of manipulation, and with the possibility of achieving mathematical standards of rigour in software development. The applicable areas of mathematics in this context are believed to be logic and abstract algebra.

Such a view is in many ways highly appealing. It offers, for example, the prospect of being able to replace the messy, uncertain and, above all, boring business of testing by a process of proof, bringing with it greater certainty about the correctness of the software. The choice of underlying theory is also fairly compelling: it is plausible to treat programming languages as being formal languages in exactly the same way that logic is, and programs as being amenable to the same kind of manipulations as logical formulae.

There are signs, however, that the recent wave of enthusiasm for formal methods is ebbing slightly, and that formal methods have not lived up to the expectations of the enthusiasts. The title of a recent workshop presentation by Tony Hoare, *How did software get so reliable without formal methods?* [Hoare, 1994], provides some circumstantial evidence for this claim. This title indicates an appreciation both of the limitations and marginality of current formal methods, and also of the achievements of current, informal, software engineering techniques.

There are many reasons for the failure of formal methods to live up to expectations, prominent among which are the three following:

1. The level of current languages. Perhaps the best known of products of the formal methods movement are formal specification languages such as Z and VDM-SL. These languages only achieve a very small amount of abstraction away from code. They abstract away algorithmic detail, but provide neither an effective way of discussing software structure nor a theory of software design. They are actually at the same level as traditional third-generation programming languages, with the disadvantage of having well-understood and effective compiler technology replaced by the more difficult and ill-supported discipline of proof.

2. The inadequacy of current techniques. Many of the benefits of formal methods are held to flow from the mere act of specifying a system formally. However, most authorities on the subject at least pay lip-service to the importance of proof, or more generally, to the prospect of being able to formally derive a program from a specification and get a guarantee that it satisfies the specification. The complexity of the proofs required for all but the most trivial problems is daunting, however, and current tools for supporting this activity are really only research prototypes.

3. Formal methods do not address what industry sees as the most significant problems in software development today. The typical formal methods development starts with a fixed specification of a self-contained system, and aims to prove the consistency of this system, and the correctness of a derived implementation. In much of the software engineering industry, however, this model of software is becoming obsolete: what is much more important is an emphasis on modularity, reusable components, distributed systems and interactive systems. Formal methods do not have a good record in these areas. For example, many attempts have been made to address the

problem of retrieving software components from a library, based on a formal specification of their interface: none have reached any significant level of plausibility.

It is likely that at least some of these problems reflect the limits of current technology and the immaturity of the subject. Hopefully, further research will increase both the effectiveness and applicability of formal techniques, and they will come to play a more central role in software development. Some formal methods enthusiasts would like to claim more, however. The quotation from Dijkstra considered earlier indicated clearly his belief that formal methods can encompass the whole of software engineering. There are good reasons for doubting this, including the following.

1. Formal methods do not address the validation of specifications. A formal specification is a formalization of a user's informal requirements, and it is hard to see how the process of checking that the specification meets the user's needs could be completely formalized, or that doing so would remove the phenomena of changing requirements, or of users changing their minds about their needs.

2. A significant proportion of software engineering is concerned with techniques for managing large-scale development, such as the study of design methodologies, project management issues, and quality assurance methods. Widespread adoption of formal methods would not do away with the need for these techniques: in an environment that developed software by means of proof rather than by coding, for example, there would still be a need for quality assurance procedures.

3. One response to the criticisms of formal methods listed above has been to emphasize the utility of formal methods in the restricted domain of safety-critical software, where there is a very heavy emphasis on reliability and correctness of code. Even in this area, however, theoretical objections have been raised. In [Littlewood and Stringini, 1993] for example, it is argued that to obtain ultra-reliable systems proof is not sufficient: it is also necessary to pay attention to the software's behaviour in its operational environment.

The topic of formal methods has been considered in detail because there has been an important and influential research programme in recent years attempting to establish formal methods as the underlying theory of software development. The discussion above can be summarized in the following three points.

1. Formal methods is an intriguing and promising area of research, and does capture some very important and characteristic aspects of software and programming. Further, there is no other significant proposal at the moment which claims to provide a theory of the appropriate sort.

2. The current state of research in formal methods does not really allow us to make a judgement on the long-term prospects of the research programme. In particular, the lack of progress in mathematical modelling of large-scale program structure is disappointing: attempts to introduce modularity into Z and VDM, for example, have merely mimicked modular disciplines from programming languages, not explained them.

3. Even supposing the ultimate success of the research programme, it is extremely unlikely that software development will ever be reduced to the sort of formal exercise that Dijkstra seems to expect, and indeed long for.

Given the unresolved state of the debate, what role have formal methods to play in current software engineering curriculums? There is a strong tendency for software engineering courses at all levels now to include a mandatory element of formal methods. The problem is that the technology does not exist to make it possible to integrate them across the curriculum and so they are often perceived by students as being an interesting but ultimately irrelevant part of the course. The argument for inclusion is that even limited exposure to formal methods will raise the general level of awareness, and that as graduates with this exposure percolate through the industry the appreciation, and hopefully the use, of formal methods will increase.

11.7   A sample undergraduate curriculum

We will now turn from the rather abstract arguments given above and examine a concrete curriculum proposal for undergraduate courses in software engineering education. In 1989 an influential report was published by a joint working party of the British Computer Society and the Institute of Electrical Engineers [BCS and IEE, 1989], the two major professional bodies in the UK concerned with software engineering. The report drew the following main conclusions:

1. Specialist courses to educate software engineers require most of the time available for an undergraduate course.

2. Software engineering requires a combination of engineering principles, design skills, good management practice, computer science and mathematical formalism.
3. The topics of *design* and *quality* should pervade the course, recurring in relation to many individual topics and creating an ethos in which students are enabled and encouraged to develop design skills, and apply engineering judgement in the selection and use of appropriate design tools and methods.

Reading the report, one gets the clear impression that its authors see software engineering as having a much wider focus than computer science. This impression is borne out by the seven skills that the report specifies as being central to software engineering:

1. System design, and the design of changes to systems.
2. Requirements analysis, specification, design, construction, verification, testing, maintenance and modification of programs, program components and software systems.
3. Algorithm design, complexity analysis, safety analysis and software verification.
4. Database design, database administration and maintenance.
5. Design and construction of human–computer interaction.
6. Management of projects which accomplish the above tasks, including estimating and controlling their cost and duration, organizing teams and monitoring quality.
7. Appreciation of commercial, financial, legal and ethical issues arising in software engineering projects.

These central skills are underpinned by seven "supporting skills": these are not specific to software engineering but represent the fundamental skills and knowledge that software engineering students ought to possess. These skills represent necessary background knowledge: students should have a general appreciation of and competence in these areas, but it is not intended that students are expert in all these areas.

1. Information handling skills.
2. Mathematical skills, especially knowledge of discrete mathematics.
3. Knowledge of computer architecture and hardware.
4. Knowledge of digital communication systems.
5. Numerical methods.
6. Knowledge of some major existing components and systems.
7. Contextual awareness.

The curriculum is completed by a list of "advanced skills", which are intended to give the experience of depth. They are presented in the form of a list of topics: many of the topics would be equally at home on a computer science degree, and their specific relevance to software engineering and coherence with the rest of the curriculum is not made clear.

The first observation to be made about this proposal is that the list of "central skills" is similar to the list of "core areas" of computer science identified in the ACM report examined earlier. The major changes are an expansion of the "software methodology and engineering" area into the first two central skills, and the inclusion of project management and contextual issues into the BCS/IEE proposal. Consequently, this curriculum also gives the impression of being rather a miscellany. This impression is particularly strong when the suggested list of advanced topics is examined. The intent of the authors here seems to be to pick topical and "state of the art" areas in computer science, rather than encouraging any depth of reflection into software engineering principles and practice.

As argued above, in the absence of an underlying theory of software development this is to some extent to be expected. More positively, many of the suggestions made by this curriculum proposal are in broad agreement with the positions put forward earlier in this chapter. For example, many of the traditional topics of computer science are present at the level of "supporting skills", indicating that it is sufficient for a software engineer to have a broad understanding and appreciation of the subject, without necessarily studying the topic in depth.

The pervading emphasis on design is perhaps the most positive aspect of the report. As the report says, design is perhaps *the* characteristic engineering activity, and it is precisely the design of large software systems that current computing theory has very little to say about. In the absence of an adequate theory of software design, however, the best that can be done is to offer examples of good practice, and plentiful case studies.

In summary, the BCS/IEE report presents something intermediate between a traditional computer science curriculum and a fully-fledged software engineering curriculum. Given the current state of software engineering theory, however, it is a very reasonable and helpful proposal.

11.8 Expectations of industry

The discussion so far has been largely from the academic point of view. There are good reasons for this: the status of software engineering as an academic discipline is still rather precarious, and the distinctive character and validity of the subject need to be argued for. However, the inchoate state of the subject also has profound implications for the relationship between software engineering educators and those in industry who will be employing the graduates of software engineering courses.

The majority of managers of software development projects have not had the benefit, or otherwise, of a software engineering education. This has two significant consequences. First, there is not a strong software engineering culture in industry today, nor any widespread adherence to what few principles of software engineering there are. Evidence for this is the overwhelming number of companies who have reached only the lowest level of the SEI software process maturity model [Humphrey, 1989]. Second, this means that industry has no clear idea of what can be expected of a graduate in software engineering, leading to many misunderstandings between academics and industrialists.

To caricature the situation slightly, industry tends to view the term "software engineer" as signifying little more than "up to date; programmer proficient in the latest techniques and languages". Software engineering graduates should therefore be immediately productive in an industrial setting. Any disappointment in this scenario is seen as a failure of education.

Academics, on the other hand, are keen to stress fundamental principles, and the existence of "transferable skills". The fact that the graduate does not know language X is not a problem but an opportunity: as a result of their education, graduates will have an understanding of the principles underlying the new language, and will therefore be able to learn and make effective use of it much quicker than would otherwise have been the case. Given the acknowledged rate of change in the computer industry, this ability should be seen as being much more valuable than mere expertise in a transient technology.

There is clearly room for a rapprochement between the two sides. Software engineering educators can play a twofold role in bringing this about. First, students need to be encouraged to keep the practical needs of industry in mind, and to be aware of the distinctive problems of real-life software development. As argued above, the ability to impart this awareness is one of the major advantages to be expected from specialized software engineering courses.

Second, there is scope for academics to make more use of the experiences of commercial software developers in software engineering teaching and research. There is a enormous mismatch between the scale and ambition of the software being routinely produced by industry, and the extent to which such developments can be analysed or managed with the aid of software engineering theory. To a large extent, progress in software development techniques is currently being driven by industry, not academia. This leads to the ironic situation of academics fulminating against the inadequacies of industrial practice, while at the same time becoming increasingly reliant on the results of such practice. Wordprocessors, the environment provided by windowing systems such as X Windows or Microsoft Windows, and developments in networking such as the Internet form the background of every academic's life, yet none of these systems were produced with the aid of the kind of methodologies so beloved of software engineers: this is made clear in the description of Microsoft's working practices contained in [Wallace and Erickson, 1992], for example.

11.9 Conclusions

This chapter has argued that software engineering education is in a transitional state. There is wide, though not universal, agreement that software engineering courses as distinct from computer science courses are needed, and existing curriculum proposals still show very clear traces of their derivation from computer science.

It has been argued that the major influence hindering the further development of software engineering is the lack of an established scientific or mathematical theory of software which could serve as a foundation for emergence of a mature engineering discipline. This lack is reflected in the rather *ad hoc* way in which software development is still carried out.

An educational consequence of this lack of a scientific basis is that existing software engineering courses often give the impression of being merely anthologies of "best practice", and are sometimes hard to distinguish from computer science courses. Despite the undeveloped nature of the subject it is important that specialized software engineering courses are offered by universities, both to emphasize the difference of software engineering from traditional computer science and also to act as foci for further research into the subject.

As the title of this chapter suggests, we are faced with a choice: to develop an adequate discipline of software engineering, encompassing both theory and practice, or to continue suffering the consequences of poorly understood and badly managed software projects. The establishment of distinct departments and courses of software engineering in universities can help this development, and hopefully have some effect on the industrial practice of software development, even in the absence of a developed theory of software.

About the author

Mark Priestley is head of the Software Engineering Division in the University of Westminster's School of Computer Science. His current research interests are in the areas of software design, formal methods and programming languages.

> Farewell, Monsieur Traveller:
> look you lisp and wear strange suits . . .
> **William Shakespeare,** As You Like It,
> (Steele, 1984)

References

BCS and IEE (1989), A Report on Undergraduate Curricula for Software Engineering.

Demiel L. (ed) (1990), Proceedings of the SEI Conference on Software Engineering Education, Springer-Verlag, LNCS 423.

Denning P. et al. (1989), Computing as a Discipline, Communications of the ACM 32(1) 9–23 (January 1989).

Dijkstra E. (1989), On the Cruelty of Really Teaching Computer Science, Communications of the ACM, 32(12) 1398–1404.

Ford G. (ed) (1988), Proceedings of the SEI Conference on Software Engineering Education, Springer-Verlag, LNCS 327.

Gibbs N. (ed) (1989), Proceedings of the SEI Conference on Software Engineering Education, Springer-Verlag, LNCS 376.

Hoare C.A.R. (1989), Programming is an engineering profession in Essays in Computing Science, Hoare C.A.R. and Jones C. (eds), Prentice Hall.

Hoare C.A.R. (1994), How did software get so reliable without formal methods?, Proof Club presentation, Edinburgh, 21 March, 1994.

Humphrey W. (1989), Managing the Software Process, Addison-Wesley.

Littlewood B. and Stringini L. (1993), Validation of Ultrahigh Dependency for Software-Based Systems, Communications of the ACM, 36(11) 69–80.

Naur P. (ed) (1968), Proceedings of the First NATO Conference on Software Engineering.

Parnas D. (1990), Education for Computing Professionals, Computer 23(1), 17–22.

Shaw M. (1990), *Prospects for an Engineering Discipline of Software,* IEEE Software, November 1990, 15–24.

Sledge C. (ed.) (1992), *Proceedings of the SEI Conference on Software Engineering Education,* Springer-Verlag, LNCS 640.

Steele G. (1984), *The Common LISP Reference Manual,* Digital Press.

Tomayko J. (ed.) (1991), *Proceedings of the SEI Conference on Software Engineering Education,* Springer-Verlag, LNCS 536.

Wallace J. and Erickson J. (1992), *Hard Drive: Bill Gates and the Making of the Microsoft Empire,* Wiley.

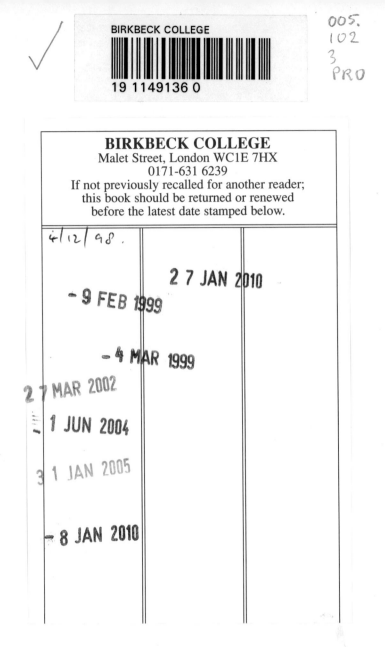